LESBIAN AND GAY ISSUES
IN THE ENGLISH CLASSROOM

Open University Press

English, Language, and Education series

General Editor: Anthony Adams
Lecturer in Education, University of Cambridge

This series is concerned with all aspects of language in education
from the primary school to the tertiary sector. Its authors are
experienced educators who examine both principles and practice of
English subject teaching and language across the curriculum in the
context of current educational and societal developments.

TITLES IN THE SERIES

LESBIAN AND GAY ISSUES IN THE ENGLISH CLASSROOM

The importance of being honest

Simon Harris

Open University Press
Milton Keynes · Philadelphia

Open University Press
Celtic Court
22 Ballmoor
Buckingham
MK18 1XW

and
1900 Frost Road, Suite 101
Bristol, PA 19007, USA

First Published 1990

British Library Cataloguing in Publication Data

Harris, Simon
    Lesbian and gay issues in the English classroom: the
    importance of being honest.
    1. England. Secondary schools. Curriculum schools. English
    literature. Special subjects. Homosexuality
    I. Title
    820.9353

    ISBN 0-335-15194-9 (paper)

Library of Congress Cataloging-in-Publication Number Available

Typeset by Rowland Phototypesetting Limited
Bury St Edmunds, Suffolk
Printed in Great Britain by Biddles Limited
Guildford and King's Lynn

To my parents for so many reasons but primarily for allowing me the space in which to realize the importance of being honest

*   *   *

To the memory of Derek Hughes

Contents

General editor's introduction

As the author indicates early in his book, a few years ago he was a student of mine on a course of initial teacher education in Cambridge. As part of his coursework he submitted a dissertation which substantially forms the basis of the present volume. At that time it had to be rewritten so as to satisfy the examination requirements, though I had no doubt that if it had been a submission for an MEd degree it would have obtained a very good grade indeed. In a curious way, the vagaries of examinations being as they are, it was too good for the level at which it was being examined.

None the less I thought little more of it once Simon had ceased to be my student until about a year ago when I was supervising the work of another student, a BA candidate this time, who was writing a dissertation on introducing lesbian and gay literature into English classes. In working with her I came to realize just how little serious work has been done in this area. I immediately got in touch with Simon to see if we could resurrect his earlier dissertation to assist my new student.

In the mean time, Simon had expanded his qualifications for writing. He is now teaching English and Media Studies in a London school where he is second in the English department and a teacher governor. He is a regular writer on lesbian and gay issues and a volunteer worker at a gay counselling and befriending centre. He has, therefore, both the educational and pastoral experience that has enabled him to see his earlier work in a wider context. We next met in January 1989 and this book is the result.

It seems to me an important book, not only for what it has to say and for the practical help it gives to the English teacher, but also because it is unique in addressing these important issues under the imprint of a serious academic publisher. As Simon suggests, it is astonishing that such a book should have to be written as we come into the closing years of the century. But in spite of liberalization of many of our values, lesbian and gay students and teachers remain an invisible minority in spite of the well-established figures for their incidence in the population, more so than that of any of the ethnic minorities for example.

Just as current educational policies are pleading for the provision of equal opportunities in other fields and we are becoming more aware of the need to educate our whole population for cultural pluralism, our legal system is doing even more to marginalize gay issues in our schools. When discussion of such issues does arise at a populist level, it is generally to use society's homophobia (especially that of the press and media generally) and to use the alleged promotion of 'gay values' to fight some other, mainly political cause. Simon's book helpfully documents some examples of these latter-day witch-hunts that are still in progress.

But since all our students will sit in class with, be taught by, and eventually work alongside those who are lesbian and gay, it is surely important that issues of sexual preference are raised with them in a serious way in school.

As with many other sensitive and controversial areas in the curriculum, experience suggests that it is very often the English teacher, working through the medium of literature, who can both raise and distance such issues so that they can be considered on a basis of empathy and understanding rather than just discussed as 'problems' requiring a clinical and quasi-sociological approach.

The schemes of work that form part of this book are examples in the first instance of good and committed English teaching; the books that are recommended in the very helpful appendix are first of all presented as worthwhile works in their own right. The fact that they are concerned with lesbian and gay 'issues' has to take second place to this. We are not, of course, dealing with 'issues'; we are dealing with people and with the sensitive portrayal of human life, feelings and aspirations in fiction, as we would in any English class.

But there is a difference. The first is a simple, but major, one of supply and availability. In preparation for writing this introduction I spent an afternoon visiting Cambridge's many bookshops with Simon's list of novels in my hand. Apart from the ubiquitous *Maurice*, sanctified and sanitized as 'an English classic' because written by E. M. Forster, my trawl managed to reveal only about ten other titles. If this is true in Cambridge, one wonders what the position is in most other towns where the provision of bookshops is often meagre. Outside London and a range of specialist shops, little is easily available. Further, in long experience of visiting schools and school libraries, I have seen very few of these titles on the shelves. This would no longer be the case with 'straight' women writers (both the Women's Press and Virago are well represented in the bookshops) and, in schools and libraries at any rate, it would generally not be the case with ethnic-minority writers. We are increasingly aware of the need to include such writers within the curriculum; indeed the report of Professor Cox's working party on *English 5–16* (DES 1984) makes a special point of this. Not so, however, in the case of gay literature. At another level we resist the use of sexist and racist language in the classrooms and playgrounds, yet opprobious epithets based on real or alleged sexual preference are the common insults of the playground in infant and junior schools.

The gay community remains, therefore, a neglected and sizeable minority, all the more easily neglected because it is not easily recognized. It was suggested by a gay writer in the 1960s that if one morning all gays woke up to find that their skin pigmentation had turned to green overnight, attitudes would very quickly change. Most students in school, therefore, even when they become aware of their sexual orientation, conceal it from themselves and others, aware of how they have been marginalized and unable to find a serious forum for discussion. This is at least as much a loss for the 'normal' student as it is for the 'gay'. The prejudices they have acquired from the society around them are confirmed, the existence of the tenderness of gay love is denied.

In providing a scholarly discussion of these issues in a context where they will be useful to English teachers as well as suggesting where necessary information and resources can be found, Simon Harris has done a considerable service. Because of its publication in this series the book will find its place in mainstream bookshops and publishers' exhibitions instead of itself being marginalized and available only from 'specialist' suppliers. This is surely right and it is hoped that it will be read and give rise to wide discussion amongst English teachers of every sexual orientation and preference.

I must declare an interest in this matter. As one who belonged to a generation when these things were never discussed in schools (to what extent have things changed, one wonders) and who was psychologically maimed in school as a result, I wish my very skilled and sensitive English teachers could have read this book. This might have saved me from a lifetime of uncertainty which, working with students like those mentioned at the beginning of this introduction and working with Simon on this book, is only now beginning to be resolved. In congratulating Simon on his achievement on producing a scholarly book so speedily and putting an important issue so firmly into the public arena, I must also add a personal word of thanks.

Anthony Adams

Preface

Much of the material used in this book originally saw the light of day in a piece of work which I produced as part of the required final assessment for a Post-Graduate Certificate in Education undertaken in 1985/6. The dissertation was entitled *Taking Away the Closet: An Argument in Favour of Positive Action in Schools to Defuse Homophobia.* Then, as now, it was written for initial submission to Anthony Adams. Four years ago he received the work as my course tutor at the Department of Education at Cambridge University; this time, I sent work to him in his capacity as General Editor for the *English, Language, and Education* series for the Open University Press.

A large part of the information and ideas contained in that essay has been rendered obsolete by both the passage of time and the materialization of three recent social, political and educational factors and their implications. The first is the appearance on the statute books of Section 28 of the Local Government (Amendment) Act 1988. The second is the now more precise, scientific understanding of HIV transmission and AIDS. The third is the transfer of responsibility for sex education to school governing bodies.

In addition to these changes, I myself have been teaching English for four years in an inner London boys' secondary school and have, I hope, fewer of the naive preconceptions which (mis)informed the original piece. None the less, a good deal of what appears in this book comes directly from that essay. Many of its statistics, examples and arguments still seem to me to hold true and deserve inclusion; for, despite the vastly increased coverage which has been afforded to this issue by educationalists, politicians and the media, there has been precious little new information and, more specifically, research published in the intervening years.

The word 'sexuality', which is used throughout this book and forms its core, ought by rights to indicate to the reader that the book will be concerned with the gamut of emotional and physical relationships which subsist between individuals. Perhaps in another society, governed by a very different set of social, moral, ethical and legal codes, this might be the case. However, in the Britain of today, such a text would be somewhat premature. As teachers of English, we are quite prepared to make use of resources which portray and reflect heterosexual relationships. (They are invariably the backbone of our GCSE teaching.) Yet few of us are really ready to accept a practical guide to the introduction of materials dealing with homosexual relationships, without some theoretical arguments to persuade us so to do.

During much of the time while I have been writing, I have experienced feelings of immense anger that such a book needs to be written at all in what is, after all, the last decade of the twentieth century. It seems incredible to me that we are still at the sorry stage where 10 per cent (Kinsey *et al.* 1953) of our students are being alienated, victimized and have to experience unacceptable levels of prejudice. Society's only response to this desperate position is to threaten any local authorities which have the temerity to attempt to ameliorate it.

However, such a book is, unfortunately, necessary and its intention is to argue that the time has now come to stop this inequality and recognize the importance of being honest. In the same way that texts, from the early 1950s onward, which were arguing for the inclusion of aspects of race in the school curriculum, concentrated on those races which had previously been ignored, marginalized or maligned, so this book uses the word 'sexuality' to denominate that sexuality which mainstream education has always left out in the cold.

Acknowledgements

Thanks are due to the following, for their invaluable help, information and advice: Alex McLeod, Paul Patrick, Cris Townley, Gay London Police Monitoring Group (GALOP), Michael Place, Alex Hirst, Mark Baker, Peter Tatchell, Simon Watney, *Capital Gay* and especially *The Pink Paper*.

Grateful thanks are due to the following for their kind permission to use their material: Peter Bradley for 'You are my good teachers', Jimmy Somerville for 'Smalltown Boy', and Amber Lane Press for the extract from *Bent*. Acknowledgement is also made to Faber and Faber Ltd for '28th September' and Virago Press for 'Lesbian'.

On a personal level, I want to thank Deborah Harris, Alice Hudson, Stephen Grant, Dave Bridle, Jacquie Mutter, Simon Woodage and my parents for their guidance, support and tolerance. I am also incredibly grateful to Tony Adams for his faith.

Finally, to all those teachers whom I have been fortunate enough to meet both informally and through different groups who are already out there doing it, while some of us are just writing about it.

1 Introduction

In my school there isn't any great discussion of relationships, homosexual or heterosexual, and I'm not sure that there necessarily should be . . . I don't think that school is the place for [homosexuality] to be discussed.

(Mr L. Norcross, then Headteacher, Highbury Grove School, London, in a phone-in debate, LBC Radio, 8 March 1984)

Although a comment made six years ago, the point which Norcross makes still needs to be addressed today. Why has this book, whose basis is the place of sexuality within the English curriculum, been written at this particular time? What possible relevance does this issue have to the teaching of English or, for that matter, education in general?

In trying to answer these questions, I see the task of this book as being four-fold. First, in this chapter I shall examine how and why sexuality has come to find itself centre-stage in the educational (and political) debate. The remaining part of the chapter then attempts to clarify some of the terms which are used throughout the rest of the book, focusing particularly on one, **homophobia**, whose very existence and pervasiveness has made a book such as this necessary. Second, Chapter 2 tries to answer Norcross by discussing why aspects of sexuality need to be tackled in schools. Third, Chapter 3 examines what the implications of this are for the teacher of English. Fourth, Chapters 4, 5 and 6 suggest possible materials, including two literature case studies for use with 15–16-year-old students, as well as relevant strategies and approaches, which might be adopted. In conclusion, Chapter 7 focuses on the potential contributions of individual teachers, including the responsibilities of lesbian and gay staff, the role of the English department as a whole, as well as that of other departments, before finally examining the place of the institution itself and that of the local education authority. The appendix comprises a resource list, which, while not claiming to be comprehensive, will, it is hoped, be useful in beginning to tackle this issue.

Why the issue is on the educational agenda and how it got there

Britain has never been a country which has been comfortable countenancing any discussion or display of sex or sexuality. It is only in the 1970s and 1980s that issues of 'mainstream' sexuality have come to be discussed openly and in the media. The emergence of a vocal lobby arguing for recognition and equality for homosexuality is a relatively recent phenomenon. Yet it is my contention that it was the emergence of three recent developments, all of which evolved *outside* the lesbian and gay lobby, which forced the issue of sexuality to the fore of political and educational debate. These are Section 28 of the Local Government Act 1988, the advent of HIV and AIDS, and the recent decision to transfer responsibility for sex education to school governing bodies.

Background

The post-war movement arguing for lesbian and gay rights can, for simplicity's sake, be traced back to the time of the establishment of the Wolfenden Committee, whose brief was to review the law as it related to homosexuality. It was set up as a result of a number of arrests of well-known men for 'gross indecency', the quaint old legal name for homosexual sex. At this time, *any* sexual contact between two men was illegal. (The law recognized no such concept as lesbianism and therefore, apocryphal stories about the ignorance of Queen Victoria aside, there was no need to legislate against it.) The committee produced its report in 1957, recommending the partial decriminalization of homosexuality (Wolfenden Report 1957). (This was ignored by successive governments over the next ten years.) The following year, however, saw the formation of the Homosexual Law Reform Society, which eventually evolved into the Campaign for Homosexual Equality. Finally, as a result of a private member's Bill introduced in 1965 and delayed for two years, Wolfenden became law.

Under the Sexual Offences Act 1967, physical relations between two men are no longer illegal, so long as *all three* following conditions are met: (1) the relations take place in a private place, (2) each of the parties involved consents to the relations, *and* (3) both are 21 or over. The direct result of the change in the law was a huge increase in openness and 'visibility' amongst lesbians and gay men and the resultant proliferation of lesbian and gay meeting-places and organizations. One such organization was the Gay Liberation Front (GLF), which was set up in 1969. Its aim was to see the extension of the 1967 'reform' into the full-blown acceptance of lesbian and gay rights across all areas of society. A radical organization, its impact waned in the mid-1970s when the majority of lesbians left, due to frustration at being marginalized by the men and their realization of the need to establish a women's movement as a more appropriate forum for their own struggles.

The remainder of the 1970s saw a lull in national advancement for equal rights, although Britain's acceptance as a member of the EEC, and that organization's subsequent ratification of the European Convention on Human Rights, appeared to bode well for all 'minority' rights. (On the educational front, less promisingly, John Warburton, a supply teacher, was dismissed in 1975 by the Inner London Education Authority (ILEA) for honestly answering a student's question as to whether or not he was gay. He was reinstated in 1981 only on the return of a Labour administration in the Greater London Council (GLC) elections of that year.)

In fact, the recent political debate itself has largely been revitalized as a result of that particular election. One of the successful Labour group's manifesto commitments had been to lesbian and gay rights, a commitment firmly rooted within the overall context of their equal opportunities package. A lesbian and gay working party was set up and further initiatives were promised. The press smelt blood and stories about the 'Loony Left' and their provision of bus shelters for disabled, one-parent, black lesbians or similar such nonsense were all the rage.

In December 1981 a new disease (ostensibly restricted to gay men) was identified and named. Acquired Immune Deficiency Syndrome (AIDS) was reportedly rampaging through the gay communities of New York and San Francisco and soon crossed the water to Britain and the rest of Europe. (Little press space was devoted to the fact that the disease had been affecting millions of people, primarily heterosexuals, in Central Africa for the previous ten years.) Rather than eliciting any kind of sympathy or understanding, the pain and misery caused by this mysterious condition was deliberately ignored by the press, in favour of 'GAY PLAGUE – WAGES OF SIN' banner headlines, whose purpose and effect was to whip up hatred and fuel violence against those who, at that point, were least able to defend themselves. The combination, then, of both the radical policies of the GLC and the advent of AIDS ensured that 'the love that dare not tell its name' was in fact being screeched from the roof-tops of every newspaper building in Fleet Street and Wapping.

In 1985 the ILEA, the only directly elected education authority in Britain, set up its 'Relationships and Sexuality Project'. Although lesbian and gay rights had been a firm manifesto commitment, it looked much more politically volatile in the cold light of day, especially having regard to the prevailing social climate. So, when the post of Project Leader was advertised, it came as no surprise that a heterosexual woman was appointed. However, Liz Dibb put together an excellent resources guide to materials relevant to homosexuality. These included both fiction and non-fiction books, films, videos and a list of useful organizations. Two thousand copies of 'Materiography no. 11' (ILEA 1986a) were duly published in late 1986 and then, three days before their launch, pulped because they contained an introduction stating that the materials were 'considered suitable for use in secondary schools . . . but should always be previewed first'. Although this seemingly innocuous clause was passed at proof stage, it was subsequently decided, at the highest level, that the ILEA could no longer stand by such a contentious statement. Two thousand new, abridged copies were printed in three days, still in time for the launch.

The Project's next venture, three videos for use as teaching aids, was similarly dogged by heavy-handed political intervention and individual acrimony, resulting in two of the videos being very heavily edited and the third being shelved altogether. The Project was ultimately disbanded in 1988, following the resignation of the tireless, but now disenchanted Ms Dibb. (Copies of the Materiography are now no longer available, although the Education Officer of the ILEA, David Mallen, gave his permission for some of its contents to be included in the appendix to this volume.)

The local authority elections in 1983 also saw a number of regional Labour groups standing on radical platforms, including commitments to lesbian and gay rights, soon to become known as the 'Positive Images' issue. One such group, which was successfully returned, was in Haringey, a small, multi-racial borough in North London. By 1985 a Lesbian and Gay Unit was in operation, charged with consulting lesbians and gay men within the community in order to assess their needs and to see how far these were currently being met by the council. In 1986, having contacted all the secondary schools within the borough, the unit produced a report which proposed the creation of a curriculum working partly to examine guidelines for educational establishments. This was approved by the Education Committee later in the same year. It was swiftly followed by local and then national outcry.

A local vicar began and then abandoned a hunger strike. More successfully an organization called 'Parents' Rights' was established. This latter protest snow-balled both locally and nationally and began to forge links with groups and individuals on the radical right, also arousing no little interest from the National Front. The group circulated a petition, claiming that the council was proposing lessons in lesbian and gay sexual practices for children in all Haringey schools. In tandem with this, the national media jumped at the chance further to throttle the 'Loony Left'; headlines screaming of Haringey's 'GAY LESSONS' were commonplace in 1986 and 1987. At the time of writing, though, Haringey's commitment has not as yet got any further than the excellent, first report of the Curriculum Working Party, *Mirrors around the Walls: Respecting Diversity* (Haringey Education Service 1988). None of its recommendations has yet found its way into schools.

As a result of the press coverage given to the ILEA Materiography and the manifesto claims of Labour groups such as Haringey and Ealing, the term 'Positive Images' became synonymous with the public perception of 'gay lessons'. Each was taken to denote some kind of indoctrination which sought to encourage homosexual experimentation amongst the under-5s! The promotion of positive images of lesbians and gay men was rarely seen for what it was: the desire to provide more honest representations than those, such as the butch Greenham Common dyke and the simpering, Larry Grayson pansy which currently prevailed. Instead, words like 'proselytizing' and 'perverted' were pressed into service to discredit the 'Loony Left'.

Throughout Britain, on a much smaller, ad hoc basis, the early 1980s saw many other local education authorities (LEAs) and individual schools adopting their own equal opportunities policies. The vast majority of these focused on race and sex, a few adding class, but a small minority chose to include words like 'sexual orientation' or 'sexuality'. Even those who had limited themselves to combatting prejudice solely on the grounds of race and gender soon came to realize that sexual stereotyping could not be seen purely as a gender issue, concerned with how men perceived and treated women and the latter's resultant position in society. Implicit in the deconstruction of 'accepted' stereotypes are the social and cultural assumptions and prejudices that exist with regard to the relationships and life-styles which reject those norms. Gradually, then, on a tiny scale and, often through the pressure exerted by a fearless lesbian or gay member of staff, issues relating to homosexuality were sneaked into the curriculum under the cloak of anti-sexist teaching.

By 1987, faced with over 1000 people dead from AIDS and possibly as many as 100 times that figure infected with the Human Immunodeficiency Virus (HIV), threatened with a number of Labour councils promising to review and, where appropriate, reform their policies relating to the provision of services to take account of lesbian and gay issues, the government decided to act; Section 28 was the result.

Section 28

> It is not the clause that will produce the backlash but the arrogant, self-assertive, aggressive boastfulness and self-glorification of a particular lifestyle which is upsetting the overwhelming majority of people.
> (David Wilshire, MP quoted in Stop the Clause Education Group 1989: 29)

The provisions and their interpretation

Section 28 of the Local Government (Amendment) Act came into force on 24 May 1988. It professed to be the full stop to a debate which had been raging both publicly and politically since 1981. Its intention, as evidenced by DES Circular 11/87, was to ensure that 'there is no place in any school in any circumstances for teaching which advocates homosexual behaviour, which presents it as "the norm", or which encourages homosexual experimentation by pupils' (DES 1988a: 22 para.). The campaign mounted by opponents of what was, at that point, Clause 28, attracted huge media attention. Marches, rallies and massive press coverage attended the often tortuous progress of the Clause, variously known during its different legislative incarnations as 27, 28 and 29, until it finally appeared on the statute book. The relevant provisions of Section 28 are as follows:

(1) A local authority shall not
   (a) intentionally promote homosexuality or publish material with the intention of promoting homosexuality;
   (b) promote the teaching in any maintained school of the acceptability of homosexuality as a pretended family relationship.

(2) Nothing in subsection (1) above shall be taken to prohibit the doing of anything for the purpose of treating or preventing the spread of disease.

What now follows is a summary of the two legal opinions, one by D. M. Barnes QC and the other by Lord Gifford QC, both commissioned by the Association of London Authorities (ALA), with special emphasis on the position for individual teachers and schools.

1 The Section affects only local authorities, not individual teachers or schools. (However, a published school policy which advocated promotion of homosexuality could well be imputed to the local authority. Equally, persistent failure by the LEA to dismiss a teacher who was involved in such promotion, might lead to the authority itself being found to be promoting homosexuality.)

2 'Promotion' would seem to require *active* advocacy or persuasion on behalf of the local authority to incite individuals to become homosexual or to experiment with homosexual relationships.

3 'Intention' is likely to be judged objectively (i.e. judging the intended effect desired by the majority of the local authority) and not restricted to the random utterances of individual councillors.

4 Local authorities must refrain from promoting homosexuality as acceptable as a 'pretended family relationship'. That does not mean, however, that they must ensure that homosexual relationships are presented as unacceptable in their entirety. On the contrary, teachers have a general duty to be honest and promote the welfare of their students. Therefore, any comments made (a) to protect any student from bullying and victimization from others who may taunt them because they or their parents are believed to be lesbian or gay or (b) any counselling of individuals in relation to their sexuality, have each been considered not to breach the Section.

5 Nothing in the Section prevents a teacher from referring to her/his own sexual orientation if that is a natural thing to do in the fostering of the relationship of honesty and trust between teacher and student(s).

(Despite this legal interpretation, a government minister, Michael Howard, has said of a teacher's reference to her/his sexuality that, 'in some circumstances and in some contexts that could amount to the promotion of homosexuality'. Even if the minister was right, it is submitted that it would be somewhat difficult to impute such a comment to the local authority.)

Implications: proselytizing

Young people at an impressionable age though *basically* heterosexual can be led into homosexuality even if it is for a temporary period. This can cause great confusion to them, upsetting their lives, their careers and their prospects of marriage.

(Lord Campbell of Croy – my emphasis quoted in
Stop the Clause Education Group 1989: 30)

A central question, which was never satisfactorily considered by the proponents of the Section, is whether *any* sexuality can be promoted, in the legal sense of the word. If Tony Gifford is correct and promotion means active incitement through advocacy or persuasion, then it would not be far from the truth to say that British society currently promotes heterosexuality with a single-minded thoroughness, verging on monomania! It, and its most obvious and accepted means of expression, marriage, is considered to be the foundation of our civilization. Advertising, literature, the media, the law: all present positive images of and favourable benefits accruing to heterosexual couples, with an almost total and obsessive exclusivity. From a very early age, children's books and magazines proffer and tempt the young reader with heterosexual relationships and their attendant benefits and drawbacks. Children are pressured from all sides to become involved in such relationships, although their sexual expression, especially with regard to girls and young women, is morally censured. But this promotion, whose sheer pervasiveness puts the glitzy razzmatazz of the British Gas share flotation to shame, still fails to win over 10 per cent of the population.

We are all brought up as heterosexual children, yet one in ten is unconvinced by what is on offer. Given the lack of acceptance and the overt discrimination with which society treats lesbians and gay men, such a rejection of the norm is unlikely merely to be the result of a choice, as easy and unproblematic, for example, as selecting the flavour of a packet of crisps. If it were, only the professional martyr would opt for homosexuality. Therefore, heterosexuality itself seems to prove the point that sexuality, of whatever character, cannot be promoted. After all, is sexuality really such a fragile, tenuous matter that it can flutter around in the winds of rhetoric, susceptible to the merest puffs of panegyric and a barrage of other less subtle techniques, all far more suited to the advertising executive?

An interesting footnote to what might constitute the 'promotion of homosexuality' is that, for several months during 1989 and again in 1990, the very government which outlawed such action if it were perpetrated by a local authority ran a series of advertisements in the lesbian and gay press. These advertisements, placed by the government quango, the Health Education Authority, consisted of two full pages. One was a useful list of HIV and AIDS helplines around Britain. The other was a three-quarter-page photograph of the heads and upper torsos of two extremely beautiful, seemingly naked young men, who are shown cuddling one another, under the headline 'If you think safer sex sounds dull, reading this might change your position'. Her Majesty's Government then proceeded to incite gay men to try the following activities: 'Mutual masturbation for instance. Fingering, massage or body rubbing.' Despite the obvious benefits of such a campaign, albeit some seven years late, it is still remarkable to see such obvious 'promotion' and conspiracy to sexual experimentation.

At a legal level, although it is of only persuasive authority in its relevance to the application of English law, a decision of the highest court in the State of New York, the Court of Appeals, is of interest. Hearing a case in June 1989, in which the owner of a rent-controlled apartment was seeking to evict the deceased tenant's gay lover of ten years' standing, the court held that a lasting, committed gay relationship could constitute a family. In the majority opinion, Judge Vito

Titone wrote, 'We conclude that the *family* . . . should not be rigidly restricted to those people who have formalized their relationship by obtaining . . . a marriage certificate or an adoption order.' The judge continued, 'a more realistic . . . view of a family includes two lifetime partners whose relationship is longterm and characterized by an emotional and financial commitment.'

In conclusion, even if the Section is in fact a chimera, seeking to outlaw the impossible, it would seem that its result, instead of curtailing existing practices which, on the above interpretations, do not fall within its ambit, has been the often erroneous, self-regulation by local authorities who have been scared away from the adoption of positive policies by its somewhat nebulous provisions. (A good example of this 'clausetrophobia' is Essex County Council's memo to directors and principals of colleges of further education warning them not to 'allow such groups [lesbian and gay] to meet on their premises because, in so doing, they put the local education authority at risk under Section 28'.) The more realistic position, according to the legal opinion prepared by D. M. Barnes, is that 'it is open to serious doubt whether it [Section 28] will render unlawful many decisions or actions presently lawful'.

HIV and AIDS

The advent of AIDS has forced local authorities and schools to tackle the issue of preventive health education in relation to HIV infection. As previously mentioned, AIDS was originally seen as an exclusively gay male problem and largely ignored in health education terms for that very reason. Despite persistent medical warnings to the contrary, it took over five years, and thousands more people testing HIV-positive (HIV+), before it was generally accepted that the virus was capable of affecting *anyone*, irrespective of their sexual orientation, who was at all sexually active, as well as haemophiliacs and those misusing drugs intravenously. Given this sudden realization of the potential scale of the problem and its grave importance, both the Health Education Authority and the Department of Education and Science begun to inundate schools with information and urgent requests that they start immediate, relevant and effective health education.

However, by the time this edict had filtered into schools, students (and staff) had assimilated so much of the virulent 'GAY PLAGUE' hysteria, which so characterized the news coverage of the first five years of the disease's existence, that homosexuality was found to be a central issue in any discussion of HIV. Teachers were then faced with a pedagogical problem. It was their task to provide students with immediate and effective health education so as to curtail any further spread of the virus. Yet this was virtually impossible until their students came to accept that it was something which potentially concerned them all. It was only once students came to realize their own vulnerability to the virus that preventive advice could be offered and stood any chance of being accepted.

Coupled with this problem were two facts relating directly to HIV itself. The first was that, despite the gay community's swift and largely unsupported response to the AIDS crisis, in the form of information and the promotion of 'safer sex' practices, any gay man involved in unprotected anal intercourse would be putting himself in the high-risk category, as far as HIV infection was concerned. So it became essential that schools' health education take cognisance of that. The second fact was that, due to the epidemiology of HIV and its mode of transmission to the USA and Europe, the vast majority of people with AIDS (PWAs) were and still are gay men, although the scale of that majority is decreasing monthly. It therefore became impossible to consider any course of health education without appreciating that it was bound to open up issues of sexuality, misinformation and prejudice. As a result, individual teachers, charged with the responsibility for such education, were forced into adopting a stance in relation to homosexuality.

Sex education

The Education (No 2) Act 1986 placed responsibility for sex education with school governing bodies who, since September 1988, have been required to make and keep up to date a separate written statement on their school's policy on sex education (Section 18). Because of this, headteachers and their staff have had to draw up proposals for the curriculum content of any programme of sex education and submit these to the governors. Because of the higher profile which lesbian and gay issues currently enjoy within society, due directly to both the public debate which led up to Section 28 and society's often imperfect knowledge of HIV and AIDS, all schools have had to make the decision as to whether or not to include homosexuality within their sex education curriculum. In theory this is an important decision, as a failure to present relevant issues to the governing body for ratification in their statement would make their subsequent inclusion in the syllabus technically illegal.

Such then are the three pertinent factors which have ensured that, however unpalatable they may be for the 'moral majority', issues of homosexuality have had to come out of their closet and be considered as never before. Before going on to look at the nature of homophobia and why sexuality has been seen as such a contentious and problematic area in the sphere of education, it is essential to state and define the often difficult terminology which such an examination requires. As with discussions of racism and sexism, matters of semantics are not merely pedantic but often can be indicative of attitude and their misuse can give cause for offence. What follows is not exhaustive but ought to explain the terms which appear throughout the rest of the book.

Definitions

Bisexual   The term which describes a person who experiences emotional and/or physical attraction to others of both sexes.

Closet   An imaginary (but none the less concrete) construct into which lesbians and gay men are forced by the attitudes, legislation and behaviour of an unsympathetic society. A closeted individual is one who has chosen or who has been pressured to maintain secrecy about her/his sexuality and consequently presents a heterosexual 'front' to and for the outside world.

Coming out
The process by which an individual comes to terms with her/his own lesbianism or gayness and chooses to be open to others about it. It is a continuing process, given society's invariable assumption of heterosexuality until proven otherwise. A person who has succeeded in achieving this can be referred to as 'out'.

Gay
The term which describes a man who experiences emotional and/or physical attraction to other men. (Some lesbians also refer to themselves as 'gay', although more radical lesbians view this as inappropriate, preferring lesbian or dyke.)

Heterosexual
The term which describes a person who experiences emotional and/or physical attraction to other people of a different sex to their own. Some lesbians and gay men use the word 'straight' to describe heterosexual people, as a direct response, although stripped of most of its parallel derogatory connotations, to the word 'bent' used by heterosexuals about them.

Heterosexism
A set of beliefs, attitudes and practices which presents and promotes heterosexual relationships and life-styles as the norm. It therefore sees such relationships and life-styles as being superior to any others and, in extreme cases, considers such alternatives as unacceptable and unnatural.

Homophobia
The irrational fear or intolerance of homosexuality.

Homosexual
The scientific term, first coined in 1869, used to describe what was then perceived (and treated) as a psychopathic condition. It concentrates solely on one aspect of human sexuality and, coupled with its clinical connotations, has generally been rejected by those it seeks to describe. Instead, the terms *lesbian* and *gay* are more frequently used. However, as there is no other generic term to describe both lesbianism *and* gayness, it is proposed to use the word homosexuality.

Lesbian
The term which describes a woman who experiences emotional and/or physical attraction to other women.

Positive Images
The term used to describe the desire to present more honest and realistic representations of lesbians and gay men. Despite the unfortunate overtones which press 'mangling' has given it, it is a useful way to describe a particular curricular objective and will be used in this sense.

The following words and acronyms and their definitions which relate to AIDS and HIV have been included, *not* because the virus is a purely lesbian and gay issue – which it quite patently is not – but because popular perception, health education and individual instances of the virus still directly affect lesbians and gay men.

AIDS   Acquired Immune Deficiency Syndrome, one of the conditions which *may* develop as a result of infection with HIV. In simple terms, it involves the disabling of a person's immune system, whose task it is to fight off infection. In fatal cases, it is *never* the syndrome which causes death, but the opportunist infections which arise as a result of the breakdown of the body's immune system and its inability to fight off those infections.

ARC   AIDS Related Complex, one of the conditions which *may* develop as a result of infection with HIV. It is generally considered to be less severe than full-blown AIDS and tends not to be life-endangering, but it does involve a significant degree of immune deficiency.

Body positive   The positive status of an individual's contact with HIV, found as the result of a blood test. Such a result indicates that the person's blood has been infected with HIV *not* that s/he is ill in any way. The individual *may* then develop any of the three related conditions: AIDS, ARC and PGL.

HIV   Human Immunodeficiency Virus, through whose infection people may (although not always) then develop any of the three related conditions: AIDS, ARC and PGL. It can be transmitted only through the medium of body fluids, particularly blood, semen and vaginal fluid, and even then only in one of a number of very specific ways; unprotected intercourse (anal or vaginal) with a person who is HIV+, sharing injecting equipment with a person who is HIV+ or the routine transfer of blood from an HIV+ mother to her foetus. (Clinical transfusion or injection of blood or blood products should no longer pose a risk in the UK at least, as these are now all tested and treated to ensure against the possibility of HIV transmission.)

HIV+   The positive result of a blood test, designed to discover whether an individual's blood has begun to make the antibodies to HIV, indicating that that person's blood has become infected with the virus. (See **Body positive**)

PGL   Persistent Generalized Lymphadenopathy, one of the conditions which *may* develop as a result of infection with HIV. It is generally considered to be less severe than ARC and tends not to be life-endangering.

PWAs   People with AIDS, which is deemed a much more preferable way of describing those who have the disease than to use words which connote a 'victim' status, such as suffering.

Positive   (See **Body positive**)
Seropositive   (See **Body positive**)

Homophobia

> It is quite right that there should be an intolerance of evil . . . I believe that an intolerance of evil [homosexuality] should grow.'
>
> > (Dame Elaine Kellett Bowman, in response to the news of the
> > fire-bombing of the offices of the gay newspaper, *Capital Gay*
> > quoted in Stop the Clause Education Group 1989: 33)

Homophobia was defined above as 'an irrational fear or intolerance of homosexuality', yet such a definition is clearly not sufficient in itself. After all, it is this concept which is at the very root of why lesbian and gay issues are *issues* at all, in a way which aspects of heterosexuality are not. It is homophobia which is the reason for a book such as this seeing the light of day; were homophobia a word empty of all meaning, there would be little point in writing about how lesbian and gay issues might be integrated into the English classroom – they would be there already. (There is, after all, little need for a text about ways in which marriage could be presented to students.) What follows is an examination of the nature, causes and scope of homophobia.

Nature of homophobia

Homophobia has been variously construed, dependent upon whether it is viewed from the personal or the cultural perspective. Therefore when talking of homophobia, it must be borne in mind that it, like racism and sexism, refers to a two-pronged concept. The first is the individual, emotional response which homophobics experience: that of fear, hatred or prejudice. The second is society's view of homosexuality in general. If this is found to be hostile, resulting in an exclusive or value-loaded presentation of heterosexuality as the norm, then it is appropriate to suggest that society's homophobia results in its behaving in a *heterosexist* way.

Causes of homophobia

> Men often hate each other because they fear each other; they fear each other because they do not know each other; they do not know each other because they cannot communicate; they cannot communicate because they are separated.
>
> > (King 1958: Intro.)

> As someone who doesn't have the courage or the willpower to follow the Bible, can I state some facts? The law and the fabric of this land is based on the Christian religion. The New Testament is based on fact not myth. Homosexuals and lesbians are not normal. Freedom of choice is an excellent idea but sometimes one person's freedom can affect another person's choice. I personally do not want to see homosexuals, lesbians or any other sexual deviants. I find them repulsive. I do not want them teaching my children, parading themselves or being in any position where

they can promote their unnatural cause, but I also do not see the point in persecuting them. I feel great pity for them and suggest they suppress their unnatural urges.

(Extract from an anonymous letter printed in the
Kent Evening Post, 12 September 1989)

The possible causes of homophobia appear to be extremely complex and it is unfortunately outside the scope of this present work to propose an exhaustive examination of them. In simple terms they could be said to fall within one or more of the three considerations of ignorance, fear and economics.

Ignorance

In this context, ignorance refers to an individual's lack of knowledge or personal experience of homosexuality. As a result, assumptions and stereotypes are pressed into service to take the place of facts, in attempting to explain away the otherwise empty words 'lesbian' and 'gay'. Thus all gay men become Larry Grayson or John Inman clones and in accord with another homophobic stereotype, a sexual threat to children, while lesbians are seen to resemble Eastern European discus throwers and only 'do it' because they can't get a man.

Fear

This refers to the effect which homosexuality has on others. There are basically two factors at play here. First, as with racism and sexism, there is that fear which arises as a result of difference in others. Many people regard themselves and their way of life as the norm and therefore view anyone who deviates from this as abnormal. They see difference as a threat and, as it is far easier to hate than it is to try to understand, they begin to clothe that fear in myths, hoping thereby to create some kind of coherent rationale for their hatred.

The second type of fear invoked by homosexuality is of a much more personal nature. There are those who see *any* discussion or manifestation of sexual expression as anathema. This may be the result of a fundamentalist, religious upbringing, in which sex was shunned as in some way impure or sinful or might, alternatively, be an attitude seemingly at variance to the accepted social mores of their culture. Modern psychiatry characterizes this latter pattern as an individual's personal sex guilt, as a response to her/his own sexual inadequacies and neuroses. Sex itself becomes taboo.

There are still others to whom the very mention of homosexuality awakens a part of themselves which they had been trying to repress, whether at a conscious or subconscious level. This reaction tends to be the preserve of the person who is still firmly ensconced within the closet. It is an often-quoted truism that people hate in others that which they most despise in themselves. For them, lesbians and gay men are queers and perverts and they themselves are, after all, normal and heterosexual. Anyway, to talk about it sensibly, would be to think about it and to think about it. . . .

Economics

As has become much more apparent in recent years, what 'right-thinking' people find so hard to stomach about lesbians and gay men is that they somehow pose a threat to the family and family life. Much of the organized political homophobia of the last eight years has centred around the amorphous idea of a return to 'Victorian values' which has found frequent expression in governmental speeches and legislation. It is too tempting not to quote an excellent deconstruction of this hypocrisy, from an otherwise unrecommended book, *Homosexuality and Education* by J. Martin Stafford (1988), an apologist for the radical right. He suggests that 'Victorian values' is a

> phrase whose ambiguity must be particularly welcome to a party which in the last five years has had a chairman who consorted adulterously with his secretary, a deputy chairman who gave two thousand pounds to a harlot (albeit not for services rendered) and a vice-chairman cited as co-respondent in the divorce proceedings of the man whom she subsequently married. Despite these facts, its unseemly posturings of unimpeachable respectability continue unabashed and unabated.
>
> (Stafford 1988: 29)

A good example of the adoption of these standards into law, as they relate to education, can be found in Section 46 of the Education (No 2) Act 1986, which stresses the need for regard to be had to 'moral considerations and the value of family life'. (It would indeed be flippant to enquire whether this entails emphasizing a divorce rate which in the UK currently stands at one in three and a recent estimate suggesting that 40 per cent of all women are subjected to incest during childhood.)

A Marxist interpretation of the family views it as the economic unit of the capitalist order. What those upholding that order object to, on a political level, is that lesbian and gay life-styles tend to produce no children, are not regulated by any socially devised structures such as marriage and that there is no automatic financial dependence of one party upon the other. Even putting aside this purely economic argument, a society which has as its basic aim, in common with all societies, its own perpetuation, can view such life-styles only with distrust and misgivings, in that they present an alternative which, if generally considered viable, might lead to a destabilization of that society. Further, lesbians and gay men themselves could hardly be forgiven for being indifferent to this, having as they do so little recognized legal or social stake in the maintenance of that status quo.

Scope of homophobia

> The men who by today's jargon are described as gay are not gay, they are homosexuals and/or buggers.
>
> (Lord Chief Justice Lane, 8 November 1983
> quoted in Greater London Council 1989: 11)

In general

It is clearly impossible to examine the extent of any society's heterosexism. As with all prejudices, it does not easily lend itself to numerical quantification. That it exists is beyond doubt and whether it results in some or a great deal of prejudice would seem to be a pedantic and spurious argument. People suffer. They suffer in all spheres of life. All of the world's major religions treat homosexuality as a sin and a crime against God. Almost all cultures deal with it as a social evil and invariably legislate against it. Those in charge of society's morals label it an 'inversion' and an 'outrage'; nowadays gay men are frequently portrayed as the aggressors in a crisis which, to date, has seen them figure as the largest single component among its victims. Employers regard sexuality to be a relevant consideration (and successive court cases have shown that a dismissal, based on the fact that an employee is lesbian or gay, will not then be construed as unfair). Lesbian mothers have been considered unfit people to bring up their own children and fostering and adoption agencies would far sooner place a child back with her/his violent parents than with a stable gay couple. Every day, from every corner, the lesbian or the gay man may experience homophobia and heterosexism in the forms of both verbal and, currently on the increase, physical abuse and prejudice which can affect every aspect of her/his life. Society, religion and culture all conspire together in their dealings with those who are gay to ensure that they are anything but. As a result, many lesbians and gay men feel constrained to live on the fringe of accepted society, masquerading as 'normal' or else are forced to choose to live separately as a community within a community.

How it affects the lesbian or gay teenager

Perhaps the two most pervasive and influential pressures brought to bear on lesbian and gay teenagers are from the media and peer groups. These factors were isolated by Michael Place (1981), while a PGCE student at the Institute of Education in London, in an innovative dissertation. Dealing first with the media and its presentation of gays and gay issues, he identified five conventions:

1 A conspiracy of silence, which shrouds the whole area. If homosexuality must be mentioned then the following four strategies show nothing if not the media's inventiveness.
2 Reference to homosexuality as some form of sick disease. This was common practice even before the advent of HIV. It was, after all, only in the mid-1970s that the American Psychiatric Association withdrew homosexuality from its list of recognized psychiatric disorders.
3 The neo-clinical press treatment of those 'suffering' from the condition. It is in this context where pseudo-scientific theories relating to cures and the supposed hormonal imbalances in lesbians and gay men abound.
4 The 'SHOCK! HORROR! PROBE!' variety of story. Here is the domain of the 'GREENHAM LESBIAN EXCLUSIVE', the 'GAY VICAR LOVE TRIANGLE', as well as the attempted media crucifixions of Peter Tatchell, Elton John and 'EastEnder' Pam St Clair.
5 The gay man as public enemy. Blunt, Burgess, Maclean, even Mountbatten, have all provided excellent copy here. They, as with Harvey Proctor, are

despised, less for their life's work and more for their life-styles. At a more bread-and-butter level, many Sunday papers are full of lesbians who desert their children and the gay men who then molest them. No consideration is ever given to the fact that being attracted to people of the same sex is completely different from being attracted to children of the same sex. Also ignored is the fact that 93 per cent of all sexual assaults perpetrated against children are inflicted by heterosexual male relatives (City of Leicester Teachers' Association 1988).

In conclusion, Alex Hirst, another student at the Institute, said, in summing up his *Report* (1983), that the effect of the media is that, 'What [public] awareness there is, is based on prejudice, misrepresentation, distortion, sensational exploitation of homophobia, prurient scandalmongering and lies'.

With regard to peer group pressure, Place (1981), dealing specifically with the gay male teenager, identifies four main factors:

1 'The society of the lads' which is foisted upon adolescent boys from all sides. To opt out is to immediately exhibit difference and bring about the torrent of abuse in which school playgrounds are unsurpassed.
2 The complete lack of other people experiencing what he is experiencing, the result of which is often the internalizing of self-hatred.
3 The requirement and obsessive desire for secrecy, in order to avoid detection of his difference.
4 The certain knowledge that even if he is able to overcome the effects of the above, the one true piece of information that he will already have, is that it is illegal for him to have any physical contact until he is over 21.

In relation to the young lesbian, consideration of whom was outside the scope of Place's work, the age of consent is clearly not a relevant factor. As to the 'society of the lads', this is also not apposite but probably manifests itself amongst girls as the stage at which they are conditioned to be 'boy mad'. A further consideration, not fully appreciated when Place was writing, but now of direct relevance, is the misinformation and bigotry associated with HIV and AIDS, whose effect upon the gay teenager cannot be underestimated. Equally its knock-on effect for young lesbians is likely to have caused a still further reduction in that already miniscule portion of tolerance or, at least, dismissiveness traditionally afforded to lesbians by society.

The intention of this chapter has been to examine why sexuality has suddenly become an issue and to locate it within some kind of socio-political context. In defining homophobia, I have sought to explain its power and prevalence and the harm it can cause. The other definitions, particularly those relating to HIV and AIDS, have been included within the body of the text, rather than in a glossary, because it is felt that this is an area riddled with semantic pitfalls and one in which the use of appropriate terminology provides a purchase against the bigotry which the concerned teacher will face in choosing to confront this issue.

2 Why sexuality needs to be tackled

Turning from those factors which have raised the issue of homosexuality to the level of regular and often vituperative public and political debate, I intend now to examine those arguments which might provide the rationale for dealing with sexuality in a classroom. Throughout this chapter, reference will be made to *Something to Tell You* (Trenchard and Warren 1984); a report commissioned by the London Gay Teenage Group, it is the only piece of research of its kind anywhere in the world. It presents and analyses the answers to a detailed questionnaire, over 1700 of which were distributed to people in London, in pubs, clubs, groups and events known to be frequented by young lesbians and gay men. Of the completed forms, only 416 were deemed to be valid, in that the respondents were under 21 and lesbian, gay or bisexual. It was these respondents who became the survey group.

Incidence of homosexuality

The most exhaustive research to date as to the incidence of homosexuality is still that of the American psychologist, Alfred Kinsey, whose findings were published well over forty years ago (Kinsey *et al.* 1947). His study, which was the result of analysing answers to a set of questions, probing the sexual attitudes and behaviour of 20,000 men and women, led him to conclude that human sexuality could be accurately represented only as a continuum, whose range extends from 0 (exclusively heterosexual) to 6 (exclusively homosexual). In simplified form, that gradation is as follows:

0 – exclusively heterosexual
1 – mainly heterosexual, with incidental homosexual experiences
2 – mainly heterosexual, with frequent homosexual experiences
3 – equally responsive to heterosexual and homosexual stimuli
4 – mainly homosexual, with frequent heterosexual experiences
5 – mainly homosexual, with incidental heterosexual experiences
6 – exclusively homosexual.

Table 1   Incidence of homosexuality (proportion of population in this range)

	Women (%)	Men (%)
Significant homosexual experience (groups 2–6)	6–14	13–38
Predominantly homosexual (groups 4–6)	3–8	7–26
Exclusively homosexual (group 6)	1–3	3–16

Source: Kinsey 1953

In 1953, Kinsey added an eighth heading:

x – people who do not respond erotically either to heterosexual or homosexual stimuli.

His research, which could be said to be statistically flawed in many ways, especially in the disparity between the numbers of men and women questioned (at the rate of 3 to 2), does, however, quantify the incidence of homosexuality amongst his sample group (see Table 1).

The large difference which existed between male and female responses may partially be explained by the conditioned reticence which women demonstrate, even more so then than now, with regard to sexual matters. This is backed up by the fact that more recent, although less comprehensive, research has tended to find that approximately 10 per cent of the population regard themselves as homosexual, regardless of gender difference. All such figures, in the very nature of their dependence upon personal honesty, take no account of those people who consciously lie or do so subconsciously, as a result of repression. For that reason, 10 per cent may well be a conservative estimate. Despite its quantifiable doubtfulness, that is the figure upon which this book intends to rely.

Who are these people?

On entering his apartment, I admit I received none of the unfortunate impressions I had feared. Nor did Corydon afford any such impression by the way he dressed, which was quite conventional, even a touch austere perhaps. I glanced round the room in vain for signs of that effeminacy which experts manage to discover in everything connected with inverts and by which they claim they are never deceived.
(Gide 1985: 4)

Homosexuals are essentially disagreeable people, regardless of their pleasant or unpleasant manner ... which contains a mixture of superciliousness, false aggression and wimpering. They are subservient when confronted with a stronger person, merciless when in power, unscrupulous about trampling on a weaker person.
(Bergler 1956)

On the basis of the figures discussed above, one in ten of the people whom we know, irrespective of their race, religion, sex, class and, most importantly, demeanour, are lesbian or gay. Between 1933 and 1945 100 000 gay men and lesbians were exterminated by the Nazis; gay men were made to wear a pink triangle so that they could be easily identified – even the Nazis realized that a person's bearing was not quite enough to indicate their sexuality. Today, only gay activists wear the pink triangle. (Lesbians wear the black triangle to remember their sisters forced to wear the badge of social deviants.) The overwhelming majority of lesbians, gay men and bisexuals whom heterosexual people encounter are invisible as such. That is because they are normal. Neither limp-wristed, simpering, affected, effeminate child molesters on the one hand, nor aggressive, butch, ugly, domineering harridans on the other, they look, talk, think and *are* just like heterosexual people. They differ in only one, almost imperceptible, respect. They enjoy emotional and physical relationships with others of the same sex. They differ from them in the same way that a woman who is attracted to short, young men, say, differs from a friend who prefers tall, older men. And neither such difference in orientation is perceptible to the eyes of an observer. Often racists can be heard to say '. . . but some of my best friends are . . . (insert name of hated race/religion)'. However, anyone saying '. . . but some of my best friends are lesbians' is undoubtedly telling the truth.

School experience

> When I began talking to individuals about their experiences it became apparent that schools had failed miserably to identify problems or to support youngsters crying out for help. . . . For those already disadvantaged by social deprivation, insecurity about their sexuality is yet another problem to be overcome before they can make the most of their education.
>
> (Hall 1988: 26)

In general

One in every ten of the students whom we teach is lesbian or gay. There are likely to be 100 of them in a school of 1000. It is reasonable to presume that they do not fare well in our schools, which present in microcosm society's homophobia. As the Hall comment above suggests, they may even be being denied access to the curriculum. Table 2 shows the results of the London Gay Teenage Group (LGTG) research, relating to the respondents' experiences at school, as a result of being open about their sexuality.

The sense of isolation, due to the individual having little or nothing in common with her/his peers, is perhaps the main problem which will affect both open and closeted students equally. *Something to Tell You*, apart from its statistical analyses, also contains revealing comments made by many of the respondents.

> I really did think I was the only young gay. (Male, 16)
>
> (Warren 1984: 29)

Table 2   Problems encountered at school

Problem	Female frequency	Male frequency	Overall frequency
Isolation/nothing in common with peers	10 (25%)	28 (24%)	38 (25%)
Verbal abuse	3 (7.7%)	29 (25%)	32 (21%)
Teasing	5 (13%)	15 (13%)	20 (13%)
Beaten up	1 (2.6%)	18 (16%)	19 (12%)
Ostracized	4 (10%)	7 (6.1%)	11 (7.1%)
Pressure to conform	6 (15%)	5 (4.3%)	11 (7.1%)
Other	10 (26%)	13 (11%)	23 (15%)
Total	39 (100%)	115 (100%)	154 (100%)

Source: Trenchard and Warren 1984: 59

Notes: Of the 416 members of the survey group, only 154 (27 per cent) reported problems as a direct result of being openly lesbian or gay at school, hence the relatively small numbers involved. What the survey does not indicate, as the result of its necessarily restrictive wording, is how many of the remaining 73 per cent of the respondents, if any, were open about their sexuality and yet experienced no problems. Of greater concern is that 32 per cent of those who were not open about their sexuality also reported having experienced problems.

> Being considered boring because I didn't want to go to parties. Not being able to talk about girlfriends. (Female, 17)
>
> (Trenchard and Warren 1984: 60)

These two quotations are representative of what many of the survey group had to say and they pinpoint the dual dilemma in which lesbian and gay teenagers often find themselves. They often believe themselves to be the only person feeling as they do in the world, let alone at school. Because of this, they firmly believe that there is nobody to whom they can talk who could possibly understand and empathize, as nobody else is lesbian or gay. Yet their homosexuality is not an issue which, once identified, is pushed easily to the back of the mind. Every day the individual will be assailed by triggers which will remind her/him of everybody else's normality and her/his own abnormality. The student may well have to lie, in order to 'keep in with the crowd', or else risk being isolated through disclosure. All social intercourse becomes dependent upon play-acting and deceit, ensuring the right reaction is offered for each situation. However, isolation and the sense of having little in common with one's peers can appear to be minor problems, compared with some experienced.

> School referred me to a psychoanalyst or psychiatrist on the pretext of 'being worried about my work'! (Female, 17)
>
> Teachers didn't know how to deal with it. I had to leave the school because of the threats. (Male)
>
> (Trenchard and Warren 1984: 61)

The organisers of the Gay Self Defence sessions in London report increasing numbers of 14- and 15-year-olds attending, after experiencing violence at their schools.

(Malcolm Dobson, 'At school', in Galloway 1983: 27)

There is little that needs to be said regarding verbal and physical abuse. They are the stock-in-trade of the racist and the homophobe alike.

People, especially the boys, kept saying: 'Poof, gay black bastard.' The usual uneducated names. (Male, 17)

(Trenchard and Warren 1984: 61)

Perhaps the most worrying statistic is mentioned only briefly in *Something to Tell You*: eighty respondents (19 per cent) said that they had attempted suicide as a direct result of their being lesbian or gay. In addition to this chilling figure, the Samaritans in a letter to the *Times Education Supplement* (6 November 1987) reported that in 1985, of all the suicides or attempted suicides of which they had knowledge, 50 per cent of those with clearly attributable motives were *directly* related to sexuality. So, transposing this to our imaginary school of 1000 students, on average 19 of them will attempt suicide because they are, or believe themselves to be, lesbian or gay. The statistics do not reveal how many others will succeed.

Position in schools at present

As was discussed in Chapter 1, sexuality has recently become such a topical issue that it has forced schools to consider their position towards it. What is not yet known is what these positions are and how they will affect lesbian and gay students. It is, I think, reasonable to suppose that the combined effect of AIDS, Section 28 and sex education will have little tangible positive impact on their lives at school. Certainly the subject will now be mentioned, probably in Personal and Health Education or maybe Biology, but generally there are likely to have been no more 'relevant' books ordered for the school library (and if ILEA and their directives regarding novels by David Rees – see p. 23 – are anything to go by, the result of the Section will have been to further defoliate shelves of books with lesbian and gay themes). Equally there is likely to have been no increase in the number of 'out' teachers whose support could be guaranteed – the late 1980s hardly having been the wisest time for a career teacher to reveal her/his homosexuality. For these reasons, the findings of the LGTG in relation to the respondents' recollections of the curriculum and the staff are, it is submitted, still relevant until such time as new research is available to document the impact of these recent developments.

The curriculum

The survey asked the sample group to recall in what subject area(s), if any, the topic of homosexuality was mentioned: 242 people (58.7 per cent) said it was not mentioned in any lessons at school. The results of the other 174 are shown in Table 3. It is to be hoped that the recent change in climate regarding the

Table 3 Subjects in which homosexuality was mentioned

Subject	Frequency	% of survey group
English	44	11
Religious Education	43	10
Biology	36	8.7
Sociology	19	4.6
General Studies	12	2.9
Sex Education	12	2.9
Art	4	1
Life Studies	2	0.5
Psychology	1	0.2
Other	14	3.4

Source: Trenchard and Warren 1984

discussion of homosexuality will have had its major impact on figures such as these. As they stand, they are thoroughly disturbing, especially those for Biology and Sex Education, subjects in which it would not have seemed unreasonable to expect at least a cursory mention during, for example, lessons on puberty or human reproduction.

> School sex education said it was perverted, that if your glands over secrete then you're gay. (Male)
>
> (Trenchard and Warren 1984: 56)

This is not unlike the sex education which Peter Ustinov received at his school. His headmaster advised a group of boys, assembled in his study, 'If you touch it, it will fall off' (Ustinov 1977: 83). Even more depressing than the statistics, and pertinent to the new situation in which students are currently finding themselves, is the fact that of those who did recall the subject being raised, 80 per cent did not find it helpful, and only thirty-five people (8.5 per cent) of those surveyed found the discussion of homosexuality in lessons useful.

The library

> During my adolescence, realising that I was 'different', I increasingly identified the need to seek out alternative means of getting information about my 'difference'. No adult could be trusted enough to be questioned; the library was the only possibility.
>
> (ILEA 1984: 50)

The LGTG research found that forty-seven (11 per cent) of those surveyed could remember their school library stocking books dealing with homosexuality. Of these, only twenty-one (5 per cent) found its contents helpful. This paucity of material is unlikely to have improved, given the current prevailing climate of 'clausetrophobia' and the press coverage which surrounded the discovery, in a London teachers' centre (not, as was widely reported, a primary school) of the picture book, *Jenny lives with Eric and Martin* (Bosche 1983). It is a book whose text, translated from Danish, presents a positive image of two gay men bringing up a child. It was only ever stocked as a resource for teachers and the ILEA had previously warned against its use with students. If the book has a fault, it is that the text and the accompanying photographs are likely to appeal only to a readership who would be too immature to appreciate the book's 'message'.

For those involved in trying to integrate lesbian and gay issues into the classroom, the book's discovery could not have had more serious effects. The press coverage and the 'righteous' indignation it engendered had a number of far-reaching consequences. The first was an overt, public distancing from any aspect of sexuality, on the part of both ILEA and the Labour Party. The second was that the issue was dragged into the realm of public debate, over a book which few would ever seek seriously to defend. Finally, the furore created by the book resulted in the media's creation and subsequent orchestration of a popular campaign calling for the curbing of the 'excesses of the Loony Left'. This, of course, ultimately found fruit in Section 28.

The ILEA, often seen as the flagship of 'trendy' issues, worried about the press backlash which came its way after *Jenny lives with Eric and Martin* and the contents of a 'leaked' letter to Neil Kinnock, blaming the Labour Party's poor perform-ance in recent polls on the public's perception of Labour as being supportive of the call for lesbian and gay rights, then hurriedly responded to misinformed calls for the banning of a novel by David Rees (1982), *The Milkman's on his Way*. Not one of Rees's best books and fairly sexually explicit at that, the book had been recommended in the ILEA's Materiography, mentioned in Chapter 1. A memo was immediately dispatched to heads and librarians and the latter were told plainly to remove the book or resign.

The staff generally

In our imaginary school of 1000 students, with a staff group of, say, eighty, we can presume that on average eight of them are lesbians or gay men. As is the case with students, they will also suffer from the homophobia inherent in schools. In many ways, it will be worse for them because, in addition to the prejudices to which students will be exposed, it is also well known that 'lesbians hate males and children' and 'gay men are all child molesters'. Consequently lesbian and gay staff will surely want to do their best to remain invisible – few, after all, would wish to tread the path of John Warburton, whose dismissal is documented in Chapter 1. (Similarly with initiatives like teacher appraisal just around the corner, it can be only the very brave or the profoundly stupid who would choose to have 'lesbian' or 'gay' stamped across their inspectoral report.) A minister for local government, Michael Howard (1987), has said of a teacher's reference to their sexuality that 'in some circumstances and in some contexts that could amount to the promotion of homosexuality'. There is little question that such a reference is completely outside the ambit of the Section's provisions, although maybe not its spirit, but who would wish to try to prove that in court?

It is then unlikely that there might be openly lesbian and gay teachers; there are few, it is true, but they do exist. The LGTG research found that over half of the survey group knew of teachers who were lesbian or gay. (However, there is nothing to show from the wording of the question how students had obtained that knowledge or whether it differed from gossip or supposition.) Of this 54 per cent, half said that knowing other lesbians and/or gays at school was helpful. Any strategy adopted to ease the plight of students ought, therefore, to take account of the needs of staff as well.

Pastoral support

It is interesting to note that in response to the question, 'Who was the first person you told of your sexuality?', none of the young women and only ten (4.2 per cent) of the men said that it was a teacher. This was the seventh most frequent answer, after friend, sibling, mother, same-sex partner, heterosexual lover and parents. Given the current emphasis so much on the school as the front-line 'problem-solving' agency for its students, this can only be seen as a surprisingly low rating for teachers and would support the point made above that many of the teachers 'known' to be lesbian or gay, were, in all probability, only presumed so to be. It surely reflects upon the levels of trust and perceived support felt by the respondents. This was borne out by what many of them commented.

> I told my teacher, who sent me to a psychiatrist. (Male, 19)
>
> The Head of Sixth Form, who warned me that I might get expelled, enquired if I had been dropped on my head as a baby. (Male, 16)
>
> (Trenchard and Warren 1984: 61)

It would appear, from the LGTG statistics, that schools and their staff are being shunned by those lesbians and gay students who are experiencing difficulties related to their sexuality. Once again, it could be argued that the situation may well have improved as a result of the recent opening up of the issue, but it is more probable that these changes will have had little practical effect. What was clearly lacking, for the LGTG survey group, was an atmosphere of tolerance and respect. It is difficult to see how the combination of HIV and Section 28 can have alleviated this defecit.

What is left, after examining the LGTG research and the more recent Hall (1988) work, is the sad realization that many schools seem to desire to shove the issue of homosexuality (and those individuals 'suffering' from it) firmly back into the closet. It is just so much hot air for those of us who talk in terms of child-centred learning, of valuing our students' experiences, if we are still not yet able to provide them with the space and the security in which to let us know that they are part of a minority group whose joint membership, after all, far outweighs the number of Black and Asian people who live in Britain.

What about kids who aren't lesbian or gay?

> I don't want my perfectly normal child learning about poofs and lezzies? What use is it to her?

Despite the unpleasant language in which this imaginary parental query is couched, it does raise a very important point. Granted that homosexuality should be dealt with in classrooms, what benefits are there for the remaining 90 per cent of students who are heterosexual? If sexuality is not transferable at whim (and the very existence of lesbians and gay men seems to be fairly reasonable proof of that), then the proselytizing lesbian or gay teacher we hear so much about is in for a bit of a disappointment. So if converts are not a real possibility, and the issue doesn't affect the vast majority of students and probably disgusts many of them, why bother?

In 1978 the Campaign for Homosexual Equality published an excellent resource pack, for use in schools, called *Homosexuality: A Fact of Life*. This title sums up the essence of the issue. Like it or not, homosexuality exists. It is an alternative life-style (homosexuality is not just about bed), which directly affects at least 10 per cent of the population and indirectly affects the remaining 90 per cent. (Directly as well, if it is considered that one in ten of their friends could be lesbians or gay and many children learn that they have a lesbian or gay parent.)

Clearly with the advent of HIV, the still prevalent misinformation regarding the transmission of the virus and those at risk from it needs to be dispelled if students are to accept their own role in the debate. Given that this will, of necessity, involve some discussion of gay men's sexual practices, few people would then argue that this should not first be contextualized by examining the relationships and life-styles which give rise to such modes of expression. It has often been said that homosexuality is not the problem; homophobia is. If that is the case, then there can be no advances made in the sphere of equal rights and equality of opportunity until homophobia is successfully countered. It could even be claimed, with no small degree of truth, that the overriding purpose in arguing for the issue of sexuality to be tackled in schools, is not so much to benefit lesbian and gay students directly but more to challenge homophobics. The question surely is do we wish to cure 'queers' or prevent queer-bashing; 'pakis' or paki-bashing? There can be no possible improvement made to the plight of lesbian and gay students in our schools, until those attitudes which seek to take them beyond the pale are finally neutered and replaced with those of tolerance and mutual respect.

It must be borne in mind that most lesbian and gay students will never come out at school. For some, the fear and trauma will be too much and they will opt instead for tacit deception, rather than risk overt confrontation. Others may remain totally unaware of their sexuality until years later. Either way, their 'invisibility' is no reason for their needs and personal development to be overlooked.

One in ten babies born will grow up to discover that s/he is lesbian or gay; obviously not all of these children will be born to parents who are themselves lesbian or gay. The genetic theory, whose thesis is the hereditary nature of homosexuality, is far from having been successfully proved and so prospective parents have no way of knowing or predicting the sexual orientation of any children which they might have. Rather than risk the 'disappointment' which

Table 4   Parents' initial reaction to knowledge of child's sexuality

Problem	Female frequency	Male frequency	Overall frequency
Good	19 (24%)	36 (23%)	55(24%)
Reasonable	13 (16%)	28 (18%)	41 (18%)
Indifferent	5 (6%)	15 (9.7%)	20 (8.6%)
'It's just a phase'	11 (14%)	9 (5.8%)	20 (8.6%)
Bad	11 (14%)	29 (19%)	40 (17%)
Terrible	6 (7.6%)	17 (11%)	23 (9.9%)
Disgust	6 (7.6%)	3 (1.9%)	9 (3.9%)
Rejection	4 (5.1%)	11 (7.1%)	15 (6.4%)
Mixed (i.e. one good, one bad)	4 (5.1%)	6 (3.9%)	10 (4.3%)
Total	79 (100%)	154 (100%)	233 (100%)

Source: Trenchard and Warren 1984: 44
Note: Only 233 of the respondents had told their parents

producing a lesbian or gay child seems to entail in our society (and Table 4 clearly documents the expressions of such disappointment), is it not more sensible to discredit any possible grounds for its arising? If homosexuality is seen neither as a threat, nor feared because of its difference, then parenting a lesbian or gay child will surely present neither problems nor misery.

In conclusion, I firmly believe that there are no rational grounds, either practically or ethically, for maintaining the present situation in education, whereby the needs and experiences of 10 per cent of those we teach are imperiously ignored, as the result either of a cowardly inertia or, worse, the unreasoned adherence to a precept from that code of 'Victorian values', the rest of whose dubious tenets, rightly deemed to be antiquated and irrelevant years ago, have been pre-emptorily jettisoned, in favour of policies based more on the dignity of the individual rather than the 'morality' of the mass, many of whom are equally incapable of aspiring to their own lofty ideals! As teachers and prospective teachers of English, seemingly so concerned with the development of the individual, we cannot begin to facilitate this if we decide, in advance, that which we consider 'appropriate' and that which we find unacceptable. It is just not up to us. We are not there to delineate and delimit the boundaries of conduct students ought to follow. Ours' is the job to create the sites in which students can respond and develop freely, unfettered by those external social pressures which seek to squeeze square pegs into round holes. So long as the actions and attitudes which they adopt harm no one, what right do society and teachers have to interfere in and scorn the lives of others, for daring to differ from their own?

3 Why English?

Not again!

Having established the requirement of tackling the issue of sexuality, the next question which could be asked might be 'Fair enough, you're right, it does seem pretty bad. Something must be done. But why, as with every other social issue, leave it at the door of the English department? How does this fit in with what we're already doing?' The intention of this chapter is to examine what it is that makes English more amenable than other subject areas in dealing with aspects of sexuality. I shall then look at students' own perceptions of English, how another issue-driven curricular development has been 'sold' to English departments and finally address other subject departments who have a role to play.

What is English? A brief restatement

Kafka commented: A book or poem must be an ice-axe to break open the sea frozen inside us.'

If you accept the fundamental truth beyond this startling image, it is clear that English is deeply concerned with the aesthetic, the creative and the spiritual. Moreover, we are responsible for helping to develop within pupils the ability to participate sympathetically and constructively in society. This must involve political, social and ethical issues and, most importantly, the ability to 'use' language with confidence – in order to learn, communicate and exploit life to its full.

(Knott 1985: 3)

English is the subject pre-eminently concerned with what it means to be a human being in relationship with other individuals, growing within a culture. By language we create the world that we need to know about, we come to know ourselves and others, we discover how to learn and how to make choices or judgements, and at the heart of these processes is responding to literature.

(Protherough, Atkinson and Fawcett 1989: 31)

These two quotations neatly paraphrase the three main concerns of the teacher of English. With a new curricular report on English appearing on what one could be forgiven for believing was a regular basis, each slightly shifting the emphasis from the last, it is surprising that the fundamental concepts underlying our teaching have seemingly remained so firmly intact. In simple form, these could be presented as follows:

1 The development of communication skills across the range of linguistic registers of reading, writing, speaking and listening.
2 The development of responses to and an involvement with a variety of texts and the issues contained within them.
3 The personal, social and moral development appropriate to each individual.

How students perceive English

In general

English as site of curriculum development and social discussion is not a notion which occurs solely to teachers. Many of our students see the English classroom as a place where concepts and ideas of a contemporary nature can be aired and examined; much of the literature which we choose to use is issue-based. It can often be difficult, on entering a classroom which has English on the timetable, to establish whether what is in progress is actually Drama, Media Studies, Social Science, History, Personal and Health Education, English or a fusion of aspects of all of them. This can mean that many students come to English prepared for a more cross-curricular approach to their work and yet uncertain as to what its specific content might be. The effect of this is that they tend to be more ready for frank and open discussion than elsewhere. With the demise of obligatory written examinations and their replacement with coursework, we are much more able to create an atmosphere in which the work set is done far more on the basis of its relevance and usefulness; even if, at the end of the day, we are aware that we are still training students to jump through a set of hoops, albeit that those hoops have been repainted.

Coupled with this is the personal and autobiographical work which English tends to require of its students. Much of what we demand of them, in the form of discursive, creative and empathetic pieces, relies on there already existing an ethos of trust and respect, allowing students the confidence and space to be able to be honest in the responses which they make. Given that sexuality is still seen as both a very contentious and personal issue, we ought to capitalize on the pre-existing relationships and raise the issue where it is most appropriate for students. Looking again at Table 3 (p. 22) it becomes easier to understand the reasons why, of the 40 per cent who recall any mention of the subject of homosexuality, just over a quarter (44 people) state that this took place in English. A depressingly poor showing certainly, but one which still supports the thesis that English is, in some ways, more amenable to the issue's inclusion than other areas of the curriculum.

Research

Within the overall context of research into the teaching of English and its effects upon student performance, there has been a small amount of work which has focused on the kinds of tasks required by teachers and the consequent expectations of students. What follows is a summary of three of the most pertinent pieces of research produced, in so far as they relate to the subject matter of this book.

What gets written about: Medway

In the summer of 1983, Peter Medway visited twenty-one classrooms in Northern England where English was being taught to 12-year-olds. He collected information relating to the 346 written assignments which had been set over the previous year and then sought to list them under a number of common-sense headings. The results appear in Table 5. Medway then tried to categorize the assignments by analysing the 'implied source of validity' required of each piece. This it was hoped would isolate the cognitive processes which were expected of the students, that is the sources from which it was intended that they were to draw in order to produce the work set. These are recorded in Table 6. Medway's research shows that, despite the totals being less than one might expect, personal accounts and reliance on students' own experiences make up 15 per cent and 28.3 per cent respectively of the subject matter and sources on which written work was based. Given these figures, Medway concludes his paper by stating:

Table 5 Categories of written assignments set

Category	%	Clarification
Fiction	31.4	
Personal account	15.0	(autobiography, personal writing, etc.)
Poem	13.1	
Description	9.0	
Fictional document	7.6	(facsimilies of 'real world' documents, reports, news stories, etc.)
Book report	7.1	
Argument	4.8	
Utilitarian/conventional	3.4	(everyday social and bureaucratic demands)
Play	3.1	
Media	2.8	
Information	1.7	(facts and information)
Unclassified	0.9	

Source: Medway 1983: 23

Table 6   Sources of validity for 346 written assignments

Sources of validity	Total	%
Experience	98	28.3
A discourse type	72	20.8
Knowledge supplemented by imagination	58	16.8
An existing fiction	37	10.7
Imagination	30	8.7
Report	21	6.1
Other	12	3.5
Idealized knowledge	9	2.6
Unspecified	9	2.6
Total	346	100

Source: Medway 1983: 33

Compared with school curricula as a whole, English in at least some of these classrooms is undoubtedly a child-centred subject. That is to say, *children are not required to pretend to be something they are not; their own honest responses and evaluations are respected and given a place.*

(Medway 1983: 37, my emphasis)

If Medway is right and 'English . . . is a good place in which to recreate and imagine experience' and is one in which over a quarter of the sources for all written assignments is the students' own experiences, then surely as teachers of English we have a responsibility to ensure that *all* 'children are not required to pretend to be something they are not' and further that 'their own honest responses and evaluations are respected and given a place'.

Versions of English: Barnes, Barnes and Clarke

A similar, although larger, piece of research, the *Versions of English* project (Barnes, Barnes and Clarke 1984), attempted to categorize 263 fifth-form assignments and place them under four general headings. These made use of the separation of topics set into those which were 'public' and those which were 'private'. The former related to pieces which tended to detach English from the concerns of everyday life, those which required their writers to stand back from social issues and put across different arguments. The latter area, the 'private', tended to be personal and domestic, chosen to be closer to the writer's own perspective. The results of this categorization appear in Table 7. The thrust of the *Versions of English* project was to argue for the inclusion of a wider range of writing tasks than those which were currently in use. However, as with Medway's research (which Douglas Barnes had supervised), between a quarter and a third (here 30 per cent) was found to indicate the amount of private, autobiographical and personal experience writing which teachers had set.

Table 7 Analysis of topics set for writing

Category	%
Public topics for discussion etc.	38
Public topics requiring personal/narrative treatment	14
Private topics (self, family, friends, school, work)	30
Subject matter not specific enough to be categorized	18

Source: Barnes, Barnes and Clarke 1984: 39

English: perceptions of 16-year-olds: Austin-Ward

Perhaps one of the most informative pieces of research in this area is a unique study which was undertaken by Brian Austin-Ward (1986) to attempt to discover the perceptions of 16-year-olds entering further education colleges, in relation to the English teaching which they had received at school. He did this by questioning students themselves. The sample group comprised 16- and 17-year-olds enrolling at seven different colleges of further education (four in England, two in Scotland and one in Wales), having come from a large number of feeder schools. The questionnaire asked five open-ended questions and the students were invited to write as much or as little as they chose.

Over half (55 per cent) of the sample group had 'liked' English at school, with the three most popular reasons being (1) the extent to which students had been allowed a say in the choice of activities within the classroom, (2) the popularity of the teacher, and (3) what was seen as the practical value that had been obtained from the lessons. The major reason cited for the popularity of a given teacher (attracting the support of 87 per cent of those who responded) was that s/he was kind, approachable and/or helpful. Of the 45 per cent who disliked English, respondents were split between those who were bored by too much creative writing and those who were bored by too much emphasis on grammar. Most of the students (79 per cent) thought English ought to be included in the courses they were following at college and high amongst the reasons for this was the opportunities which would be available for them to speak, express their opinions and air their views.

What the research seems to show is our reliance, as teachers of English, on students basing much of what we ask them to do on their own personal experiences. Given this, and their apparent belief that that is what English should be about, it is plainly ludicrous if 10 per cent of the students we teach are effectively denied access to the curriculum, because they believe or are aware that their personal experiences are not valued.

Where do 'issues' fit in? A model for gender

If the three premises listed on p. 28 are accepted as the 'core' of what English teaching is about, it becomes easier to understand why our classrooms have so often been the major springboard for issue-based curricular development. Such initiatives, which have focused almost exclusively on the fields of race and gender, have often been at the forefront of the conceptual and political armoury of 'progressive' education authorities. None has been better resourced, more productive (in terms of materials issued) nor villified quite so persistently as ILEA. Specialist inspectorates, working parties and advisory staff have all been established and funded to bring individual institutions and employees into line with the authority's programmes. It could be argued that in its policy-making heyday, the situation was easier for ILEA than for other education authorities. Not only was it the largest in Europe, but also it was directly elected by the people whom it served. Therefore an election victory could be taken as a vindication of past measures and a partial referendum on manifesto issues. For these reasons it is instructive, I believe, to examine how it sought to make the leap between the political and the pedagogic.

To date ILEA has published, through its English Centre, three separate discussion documents, aimed specifically at English departments across all sectors of the service. Each booklet, running to 100 or so pages, contains articles designed to provoke discussion of existing work and giving examples of suggested recommended resources, often supplemented by individual teachers' experiences of using them, designed to inform subsequent practice. They are *The English Curriculum: Race* (ILEA 1983), *The English Curriculum: Gender* (ILEA 1984) and *The English Curriculum: Class* (ILEA 1988). Each contains an introduction (all of which use similar wording) which seeks to integrate the issue under consideration into the context of English teaching. It might be useful to see how issues of prejudice have been 'sold' to ILEA English departments. What follows is a fairly lengthy extract taken from the introduction to *The English Curriculum: Gender*; this is particularly relevant because where authorities and institutions have adopted positive stances in relation to lesbian and gay issues, the majority have decided to see it as some kind of extension of their anti-sexist commitment, recognizing that sexual stereotyping extends right across gender barriers and adversely affects anyone not conforming to the perceived norm.

ANTI-SEXIST ENGLISH

The best of English teaching has always recognised the validity of the child's experience. It has understood that children are not vacant and passive recipients of knowledge; they must engage actively with the business of English, and bring their experiences of language and the world to bear on it, in order for successful, enjoyable and worthwhile learning to happen.

What is the business of English? Fundamentally, the processes of language. Language, however, never exists in a vacuum. It must be about something, and it must be presented and received in a certain form. Equally, language itself profoundly influences the something which it is about, and the form in which it is presented. Language, idea and form exist in any utterance in a mutually affecting relationship with each other.

(ILEA 1984: 5)

Once again, there are the three central issues about which English is presumed to be.

For these reasons, English teaching is never a neutral activity. In our choice and treatment of literature, for example, we are making and communicating assumptions and judgements. Whatever we do, we represent, implicitly or explicitly, beliefs and values which may be social, cultural or political.

We have made and will continue to make assumptions and judgements about issues of gender and anti-sexism. For example when addressing these issues we have often focused on girls and women and looked at ways to strengthen their position in relation to men and boys. Whilst this is necessary and must form an important part of our approach, we must recognise the strength which girls and women already possess and the contribution they already make. In doing this it becomes necessary to sharpen our definition of 'anti-sexism' in relation to 'equal opportunities'. For too long 'equal opportunities' has been regarded as something which girls and women achieve only when they compete successfully with boys and men, almost invariably on their terms. An anti-sexist perspective must also ensure that boys are given the opportunity to examine themselves, not necessarily in terms of their relationship with girls or their attitude to girls, but in terms of their own effective domestic and social lives. It is therefore essential that *all* teachers, whether in mixed or single-sex schools address these issues.

(ILEA 1984: 6)

If the words 'girls and women', 'boys and men' and 'anti-sexist' are replaced with 'lesbians and gay men', 'heterosexuals' and 'anti-heterosexist' respectively, the paragraph above suddenly takes on a potency and a methodology against which teachers, already committed to anti-sexism, will find it very difficult to argue. Read with these alterations, it far supersedes anything which has so far been suggested under the heading of Positive Images. That section of the introduction ends with the following two paragraphs:

If we list some of the plain categories which make up English – reading literature, writing imaginatively, writing discursively, talking in groups, the study of language, the study of the mass media, for example – we can see in general terms how an anti-sexist dimension to our teaching has obvious appropriateness to the subject. That is not to suggest that incorporating the dimension in a practical way is therefore an easy task.

In developing anti-sexist English we not only have to provide materials and resources which can be used to raise gender issues but also we must develop an anti-sexist perspective which informs all the work we do, so gender and anti-sexism become deliberate and permanent features of our work.

(ILEA 1984: 6)

Again, that paragraph, if read as relating to sexuality, goes way beyond any concept of Positive Images, postulating instead a radical integration of the issue into all aspects of English work. The final section of the introduction addresses the means through which the issue can best be approached.

STYLE AND ORGANISATION

In terms of teaching style and classroom organisation, there are connections between good English practice and the secure structure pupils need within which to discuss and evaluate their own perceptions of sex-differentiation and social conditioning.

These connections include, space for dialogue and collaboration between pupils; avoidance of divisive competition; a context in which pupils can express both a unique and a collective identity; an expert facilitator (the teacher) who knows that best results are achieved by talking with, rather than at, the pupils, and that in real educational interchanges the teacher always learns as much (though not necessarily the same thing) as the learner. At the same time, an extreme of 'neutrality', when the teacher offers no opinions or information, for instance in a discussion where sexist views – whether through ignorance or maliciousness or both – are being expressed, will not make for openness or freedom of debate, but their opposites. English teachers have a clear responsibility to *promote* and articulate anti-sexism in their classrooms, and the difficult task of carrying out this responsibility in an unequivocal, though not authoritarian or punitive way.

(ILEA 1984: 6, my emphasis)

It could well be argued that this introduction was never intended to extend to English teaching and sexuality and to quote it here is both manipulative and fraudulent. There are two points, however, which mitigate against such a charge. The first is that the same introduction, with the obvious substitution of issue-specific words such as 'race', 'multi-cultural' and 'racism', had already appeared in *The English Curriculum: Race* two years previously. This tends to support the argument that such an introduction says less about the individual manifestation of prejudice under discussion and more of ILEA's conception of the uniform nature of discrimination, in terms both of its philosophy and the methods appropriate for its defusion.

The second point which validates reference to the introduction is ILEA's own statements of intent elsewhere. The preface to *The English Curriculum: Gender* makes it quite clear that the booklet constitutes 'one of a series of resource and discussion documents on the English Curriculum'. The anti-sexist statement itself, which is the source and basis of ILEA's policy on gender, begins

The Inner London Education Authority is committed to achieving an education service which provides equality of opportunity and freedom from discrimination on the grounds of race, sex, class, *sexuality*, or disability in both education and employment.

(ILEA 1984: 9, my emphasis)

Further, ILEA had already chosen to include issues of sexuality as part of its own internal equal opportunities package.

It is contrary to the Authority's Equal Opportunities Policy to discriminate against lesbians and gay men, either directly or indirectly. Any such discrimination is considered a breach of this policy and may result in disciplinary action.

(ILEA Equal Opportunities Code of Practice, p. 12)

The first three grounds of discrimination – race, sex and class – have all received the English Centre 'booklet treatment'. The document on class was in preparation when the government introduced legislation to abolish ILEA and devolve all responsibility for London's education to the constituent boroughs in April 1990. (A cynic might argue that only Mrs Thatcher would choose the date of abolition to coincide with the end of a tax year rather than the end of an academic one!) Even had it not reneged on its original commitment to lesbian and gay issues, as outlined in Chapter 1, there would have been little point in ILEA's expending any further time, human resources and money on new curricular developments for what was to be little more than a year's further existence. That such a commitment did exist, albeit briefly, is evidenced by the establishment of the Relationships and Sexuality Project which is described in the introduction to the anti-sexist statement as one of a list of groups, 'formed to assist and resource the development of such policies'. (The history of the ill-fated project is also charted in Chapter 1.)

Implications for sexuality

While not wishing wholeheartedly to adopt the ILEA position on sexism as an exemplar statement for sexuality, it does provide the methodology for its introduction into an English curriculum. Perhaps it is most valuable in what it says about the assumptions on which current English practice is based. It isolates five such premises and I shall now briefly examine each of these and discuss their implications for a policy geared towards raising lesbian and gay issues in the classroom.

What students bring to English

Much of our everyday practice is underpinned by the implicit assumption that students are not empty vessels waiting to be filled by teachers, masquerading as fountains of knowledge. We are aware that students exist and experience things outside school and that generally those influences and situations have a more pervasive and effective result on them than most of what we try to do. So it becomes essential (and mutually beneficial) that we take account of and show an interest in these influences and experiences, if we are not to alienate students and if we truly desire to engage them actively in our lessons. To involve students in unfettered and free discussions of issues, concepts and beliefs raised by the materials with which we present them, they must be secure in the knowledge that their views and comments will be treated as of value *per se* and also as being valid to that work. Good English teaching is therefore about, and only possible as a result of, the formation of honest and trusting relationships between teacher and students and between the students themselves.

It follows that given the broad spectrum of human experience and the range of attitudes which exist, many children will hold views and subscribe to values which may well differ greatly from our own. It is not our function to persuade them of the error (as we see it) of their beliefs and instead lead them on to the path of Universal Truth. That, after all, is indoctrination. (Whatever may be our own views on arranged marriages, it would clearly be inappropriate to try to persuade the Hasidic and Muslim students we teach to fly in the face of their culture and their families.) However, many of us will draw the line at comments and actions of students which in our opinion adversely affect the rights or well-being of other students, even if that behaviour is the result of a deeply held belief and, instead, we will seek to impose our own moral/ethical code. In defence of such seeming dogmatism, it is argued that the rights of an individual ought not to be sacrificed in the exercise of another's freedom. As the introduction to *The English Curriculum: Gender* puts it

> At the same time, an extreme of 'neutrality', when the teacher offers no opinions or information, for instance in a discussion where sexist views – whether through ignorance or maliciousness or both – are being expressed, will not make for openness or freedom of debate, but their opposites. English teachers have a clear responsibility to promote and articulate anti-sexism in their classrooms, and the difficult task of carrying out this responsibility in an unequivocal, though not authoritarian or punitive way.

(ILEA 1984: 6)

That aside, surely we are aiming to assist each of our students towards the achievement of her/his own self-realization, whether the choice which they make accords with our own or not. Therefore we must accept and come to value the fact that 10 per cent of our students are or will come to identify themselves as lesbian or gay. Even if we wanted to, we are not able successfully to promote hetero-sexuality – at its most extreme, aversion therapy is still a long way from showing itself to be an effective 'cure' – and so we either choose to include that 10 per cent in our policy of valuing our students or we will continue to deny them full access to the curriculum.

Materials we use

Every comment we make, every text we use, involves the transmission of some value or belief. Just by walking into a classroom, I am implying that, as an adult, I have, first, a right to be there, and second, some power once there. Even the most unsophisticated student will pick up on both of these, although s/he may not have the resources to articulate them. If I choose to wear a wedding ring, I am saying that I support the convention of marriage, in much the same way as I would be advertising my conformity to any other social institution by wearing its badge. Similarly my mode of dress will tell students much about me and the values I hold to be important. There can never be a concept of neutrality in teachers who, despite the scepticism of some of their students, are human and therefore partial.

It follows that, in the choice of materials we use in our classrooms, we are making a range of unspoken statements as to its suitability in terms of form and content. Bringing in a class set of *Boys from the Blackstuff* implies that it is an enjoyable set of plays, that it raises issues which we believe are important and of interest to the students and that it has some 'literary' merit. The implicit messages contained in our materials do not stop, however, with their initial presentation. Having read the *Blackstuff* scripts, unless attention is drawn to their representation, we will find that the plays will have reinforced many of the negative views which some students already had about women, particularly those women in authority. Yet few teachers, nowadays, would allow Bleasedale to 'get away' with that and would devise work to highlight how much of the plays rely on stereotyping. Not to do so would be as culpable as, when reading *Of Mice and Men*, ignoring the attitudes held by the other inhabitants of the ranch to Crooks or, for that matter, Curly's wife.

Yet many English teachers will allow students to spend five years in their classrooms and think nothing of having used several love poems, none of which presents a lesbian or gay perspective, will have read a dozen or so novels and plays dealing with relationships, not one of which has a lesbian or gay protagonist. What values are being transmitted here? To ignore the issue and rely instead on the 'caring and concerned' ethos which the teacher has striven to create, is to sidetrack the issue and opt out in the same way as does the teacher who, while vociferously avowing concepts of anti-racism, none the less chooses not to use any Black or Asian writing in the course of her/his teaching.

Dual nature of discrimination

> An anti-heterosexist perspective must also (as well as seeking to implement an equality of opportunity for lesbian and gay students) ensure that heterosexual children are given the opportunity to examine themselves, not necessarily in terms of their relationship with lesbian or gay students or their attitude to them, but in terms of their own affective domestic and social lives.
>
> (Word-for-word reproduction with the transposition of gender-specific terms for those pertinent to sexuality from the introduction to *The English Curriculum: Gender*, ILEA 1986b)

Any instance of prejudice which we decide to challenge is made up of two strands. The first is the formation and utterance of the pre-judgment itself and the second is the effect which it then has. As stated in Chapter 2, there are those who are the subjects of prejudice, the perpetrators, and those who are its objects, the 'victims'. What we must decide is which we hope to cure, the 'queer-basher' or the 'queer'. We must be clear that to raise the issue of sexuality in the classroom is not only for the benefit of the lesbian or gay students as 'victims' (after all, is that to be the full extent of our dealings with them?), but also for those other students who, as a result of the prejudice which they manifest, are doing both themselves and the lesbian and gay students a disservice.

Appropriateness of methods of English teaching

However the national curriculum wishes to view it, it will be hard pushed to locate a body of knowledge which is 'English'. True, there are a number of skills in which students ought to acquire competence, but there are no substantive facts which they must learn. For this reason, the English department is (and will probably remain) one of the most autonomous in the school. Even the arrival of GCSE has extended this, focusing, both in literature and language, on a range of objectives which candidates need to attain in order to justify the award of particular grades. The 'text' in literature syllabuses, so long as it is deemed to be of sufficient depth to make these objectives attainable, has become subordinate to the tools of comprehension, response and analysis required to meet the specific grade criteria. Form seems finally to have won over content.

Teachers are now – school budgets permitting – much more able to select texts which are relevant to the needs of their students, are 'reader friendly' and raise contemporary issues in a way which was practically impossible with those texts which used to form the old GCE canon. We can bring into our classrooms the poems of Benjamin Zephaniah not only because they need to be deconstructed and anlaysed to be understood, in much the same way that a *Golden Treasury* poem might, but also because they portray everyday life from a Black British perspective. It has been said that a good teacher could produce a fine series of English lessons using a telephone directory. How much more effective are those lessons based around materials reflecting the whole spectrum comprising the human condition. Creative, discursive and empathetic writing, to say nothing of the oral work which we do, are all areas which can be highly amenable to the use of stimuli based around issues of sexuality. In Chapter 4 I shall look more closely at possible strategies which might be adopted in different spheres of English work, while Chapters 5 and 6 contain case studies for two teenage novels.

Integration

Heterosexism was earlier defined as 'a set of beliefs, attitudes and practices which presents and promotes heterosexual relationships and life-styles as the norm. It therefore sees such relationships and life-styles as being superior to any others and, in extreme cases, considers such alternatives as unacceptable and un-natural.' To achieve any success, the decision to challenge such prejudice must involve the clear determination to develop an anti-heterosexist methodo-logy in all of our work. It is vital to clarify that such a stance in no way involves becoming 'anti-heterosexual', any more than the adoption of an anti-racist position requires or, indeed, benefits from becoming 'anti-white'. It is merely those dominant attitudes of exclusivity and tacit supremacy of heterosexuality which are under fire, not those who are themselves heterosexual.

For that reason, our aim in deciding to tackle concepts of sexuality in our teaching can never be fulfilled merely by choosing to read a play with a lesbian theme. That is to give that course of 'gay lessons', which the tabloid press erroneously accused Haringey Council of doing. Instead, we need to decide to challenge the heterosexist assumptions which exist within society and which manifest themselves in homophobic discrimination. Studying *To Kill a Mockingbird* with 15–16-year-olds will do little to combat racism, if it is the sole occasion when that issue is raised and if the underlying basis of all their other work and the ethos of the classroom is implicitly racist. The task is surely to develop a perspective which reflects upon all the work we do, so that countering and diffusing heterosexism and homophobia become, as with racism and sexism, a principle and an objective upon which all our practice should be rooted. Clearly this will not mean that it has to be mentioned constantly. But once it forms part of the philosophy underpinning our pedagogy, it will inform what we teach, why we are teaching it and the methods used in that teaching.

In this chapter I have attempted to demonstrate the appropriateness of the English classroom as one of the most ideally suited sites for defusing homophobia. I began by examining the 'bread-and-butter' of English teaching, both in terms of what we ask students to produce in the form of written work and what they themselves expect from their lessons. The purpose here was to show that what we currently ask students to bring to our lessons differs in no way from what would be required were a positive policy in relation to homosexuality to be pursued. Equally, the students in Austin-Ward's study seemed to want to have taken a more active part in their English lessons while at school and were looking forward to English at college allowing them the opportunity to express their own views and ideas. I then turned to how ILEA has sold other 'isms' to English departments, concentrating specifically on ILEA's anti-sexist policy and making three central points. First, it has traditionally been the English classroom which has been in the vanguard of issue-based curriculum development. Second, according to a close reading of ILEA documents pertaining to race and sex, the strategies for fighting prejudice in these areas goes way beyond what even the popular press accused Haringey of hoping to achieve through its Positive Images campaign. Third, having regard to the almost identical introductions which each of these documents contains, it is myopic not to realize that ILEA saw that the individual manifestations of discrimination and prejudice (whether they were on grounds of race, sex, class or sexuality) could be comprehended fully and fought effectively only when they were perceived merely as separate weapons in that armoury of divisive implements, through which power and privilege are gained and maintained.

It is both naive and statistically unproved to suggest that English is the favourite subject for most school students and that they have a better relationship with their English teacher than that which they enjoy with other teachers. However, the limited research which does exist tends to indicate that students *do* expect a wider range of tasks and subject matter from English lessons and accept that they need to bring more of themselves, their experiences and opinions, than they would to many other lessons. My contention is that we exploit these factors and bring the pre-existent atmosphere of individual validity and openness to a variety of ideas to bear on the subject of homosexuality. If English is to be seen as 'encompassing the whole spectrum of human experience', then to consign any discussion of homosexuality solely to the subject areas of Biology, Personal and Health Education or even Religious Education is to imply that it must somehow fall outside the scope of 'normal' experience, and, in the case of the first two, can be seen only to reinforce the scientific, clinical approach already so prevalent.

The role of other subjects

Clearly the implications of an isolated initiative instigated by a well-meaning English teacher or even by the entire department will only serve to marginalize the issue and estrange that individual or the department. In an ideal world, the school and/or the local education authority would be involved through the existence of a policy document. (Wider support such as this is considered in Chapter 7.) However, because of the recent developments outlined in Chapter 1, discussions about sexuality are now likely to feature in other subject areas; what now follows is a brief outline of which these might be, the implications and contributions possible, both on an individual and a cross-curricular basis. I propose to examine the role of the departments responsible for the following areas: Science and/or Biology; Religious Education; Personal and Health Education; Sex Education; Social Science/Studies; History; and the School library. (The involvement of Drama and Media Studies is discussed within the overall context of the English department in Chapter 4.) This somewhat eclectic inclusion of certain subject areas, and the apparent exclusion of others, is not intended to suggest that those others have little or no contribution to make. It is just that it is easier to appreciate how these subjects selected might become directly involved. Because I am not qualified to make detailed curricular suggestions, I have limited myself to the realms of the obvious and the possible.

Science/Biology

Part of any courses of Science or Biology work will include some discussion of human reproduction. There is every opportunity here to explain that sexual expression and sexuality are not fixed norms of behaviour, but are subject to the same variety which exists in other areas of human experience. This is an excellent place to use Kinsey's (1947; 1953) research findings. Equally, homosexuality is found elsewhere in nature and to mention this can deflate the 'it's not natural' argument. Although this borders on territory more appropriate to Sex Education, it might also be worth pointing out that as sex is not just about procreation, homosexuality can be seen merely as another example of non-reproductive sex. Such a discussion also ought to make it clear that biological parenting is not the sole human *raison d'être* and that to be part of an intended conception ought to be a choice. Issues of contraception, which are implicit in much of what has been mentioned, will also need to stress that, in most sexual encounters outside long-term relationships, the condom is the *only* sensible and reliable method of viral protection, as well as being a useful means of non-chemically harmful birth control. Finally, in any work which focuses on puberty and adolescence, the Biology teacher has ample opportunity to dismiss the scientifically unproven belief that many people experience a homosexual phase which they subsequently outgrow.

Religious Education

All the world's major religions view homosexuality as a sin and it might be instructive to look at why this might be. Work on sexuality could be slotted into a general framework of how faiths have reacted to the challenge from the more open and frank attitude to sex which often characterizes contemporary Western societies. Recently the Church of England General Synod reviewed its stance on lesbians and gay men, both as congregants and within the clergy itself. Any work on marriage or other types of human bonding could include homosexuality. As an example, some radical branches of established faiths are now prepared to countenance homosexual 'marriages'; how this change has been squared with orthodoxy might well be of interest. Can one retain one's faith while leading a lesbian or gay life-style?

Personal and Health Education (PHE)

One of the newer areas of curriculum development, this subject, as well as providing an effective Health Education, is designed to prepare students for life in the real world, by equipping them with the necessary confidence and skills to make appropriate choices, to utilize available opportunities and to be able to relate effectively on an interpersonal basis. Currently this is where the bulk of HIV and AIDS education seems to be taking place. Work on decision-making can examine the role of peer group pressure and demonstrate suitable strategies designed to foster the development of autonomy in an individual's opinions and beliefs.

A major part of many PHE programmes is relationships. It is preferable (and perfectly possible) to use non-sexuality-specific terminology and to ensure that all materials presented are not based on the heterosexist assumption that all students will forge relationships with people of the opposite sex. Emphasis can also be given to the idea that all types of personal relationships ought to be based on foundations of equality, not power, and ought to be mutual, rather than exclusive. Here would also be a good place to examine the gender roles which society foists upon children from an early age. Work on the rights of the individual could include an examination of the age of consent as it affects gay men, comparing it to that for heterosexuals. There could also be discussion of the difficulties which lesbian mothers experience associated with the custody of their children.

Sex Education

Under the Education (No 2) Act 1986, Section 46, those responsible for sex education must ensure that it 'encourages pupils to have due regard to moral considerations and the value of family life'. The DES advises that the aims of any sex education programme should be to present 'facts in an objective and balanced manner' (DES 1988a: para 19). However, and seemingly in direct conflict with what has gone before, the circular continues 'there is no place in any school any circumstances for teaching which advocates homosexual behaviour, which presents it as the *"norm"* or which encourages homosexual experimentation by pupils' (DES 1988a: para 22, my emphasis).

The nebulous provisions of Section 28 pale into insignificance when compared with this welter of legislation and advisory statutory instruments, designed to regulate the discussion of homosexuality within courses of sex education. It is also clear that there is ample scope for much confusion where, on the one hand, teachers are reminded to present 'facts in an objective and balanced manner', while, on the other, are specifically forbidden to present homosexuality as the 'norm'. What constitutes the 'norm', as with what can be construed as 'natural', is a highly subjective matter. To treat homosexuality in an 'objective and balanced manner' is surely to avoid such emotive terminology. (After all, nothing is more 'normal' or natural' to a lesbian than her lesbianism.) Section 28 itself provides its own difficulties in relation to sex education. Section 28 (subsection 1) of the Local Government Act 1988 sought to outlaw a local authority from 'promoting' both homosexuality and its acceptability as a 'pretended family relationship'. Yet the next subsection, 28(2), provides that 'nothing in subsection (1) above shall be taken to prohibit the doing of *anything* for the purpose of treating or preventing the spread of disease' (my emphasis). (Presumably that 'anything' might include peeling away the layers of discrimination which shroud the issue of homosexuality so as to allow students to see HIV and HIV-related illness as potentially affecting them all.)

What all this legislative activity indicates, however, is the realization of the virtual impossibility of producing a contemporary programme of sex education which takes no account of homosexuality. One of the ironies of HIV is that it has coerced an extremely reticent society into discussing homosexuality, at a time when the virus itself was busy radically altering the lives and life-style of many gay men, who were its first port of call in Britain. The unavoidable response to HIV and the popularization of lesbian and gay issues by a number of Labour-controlled local authorities have both ensured that homosexuality can now hardly fail to be included in school sex education courses. It has become a contentious subject, as evidenced by the fact that most soap operas now boast their own homosexual: surely the ultimate proof of the issue's social currency!

For these reasons, and given their vocal commitment to 'Victorian values', the present government has sought to restrict the kind of presentation which can be afforded to the issue in sex education courses. In response, what such programmes must attempt is somehow to tread an unnecessary tightrope which stretches between, on one side, the intolerance and moralistic cant which pervades the spirit (and very often the fabric) of the legislation and, on the other, the pressing need to present objective and balanced facts which force *every* student to accept her/his potential risk from HIV infection.

Social Science/Studies

If Social Science is that discipline concerned with aspects of human behaviour and groupings, the exploration of stereotypes, the construction and operation of social structures and the consideration of contemporary sociological issues, then it is hardly surprising that this is the area where most of the pioneering work relating to the integration of lesbian and gay issues into the curriculum is taking place. Conventions such as the family, marriage, rites of socio-religious initiation are all susceptible to a course which presents alternatives to the generally accepted mores. Equally, the evolution of specific, same-group ghettos, as well as the operation of discrimination as a tool of social control, would both make useful spheres of study.

History

Perhaps the main area where History might broaden its scope is in its teaching of the Holocaust. All too often, the unspeakable horror of the attempted genocide, the systematic and unparalleled destruction of 6 million Jewish people, results in the Jews' being perceived as the sole victims of the Nazi extermination programme, as they were in its initial establishment. Yet the concentration camps, the crematoria and the hastily dug pits were responsible for the deaths of *10* million people. The remaining 4 million processed by the macabre death machine were made up of travellers (gypsies), those differently abled, nationals from conquered territories and an estimated 100 000 gay men and lesbians. All of these people also deserve to be remembered and mourned.

The sexuality of great figures in history – Plato, Aristotle, Edward II, James I, and so on – is relevant, if for no other reason than to make the points that homosexuality is not a new-fangled contemporary 'fad', that the isolated student sitting in the classroom is not the only person ever to be homosexual and, further, that it is quite possible to lead a full and positive life as a lesbian or gay man.

Finally, it is difficult to envisage how a study of ancient Greek civilization could be approached without examining its attitudes to homosexuality, which were so central to and had such a pronounced effect upon its culture and politics.

The School Library

> During my adolescence, realising that I was 'different', I increasingly identified the
> need to seek out alternative means of getting information about my 'difference'. No
> adult could be trusted enough to be questioned; the library was the only possibility.
> (ILEA 1984: 50)

This quotation, which appeared in Chapter 2, neatly summarizes the role which a good school library has to play. Clearly it should stock a wide variety of books, both of fiction and non-fiction, in which the subject matter of homosexuality is well represented. Information about relevant help-lines and local youth groups should also be available. As with anti-sexist initiatives, resources ought not to be classified or 'targeted' on the basis of the presumed gender or sexuality of the reader.

The major problem in achieving all of this, however, is that books in libraries have been the cause of some of the worst homophobic storms to date, certainly in so far as education is concerned. As was documented in Chapter 2, it was the discovery, ostensibly in a primary school library but, in fact, in a teachers' centre, of *Jenny lives with Eric and Martin* which sparked off a huge furore both within the press and the ILEA hierarchy itself. To their detriment, ILEA then acceded to politically well-timed but none the less bigoted requests for the removal of a novel by David Rees, *The Milkman's on his Way*, from their library shelves (see p. 23). In addition to this, 'clausetrophobia' or at least its self-regulatory element is also likely to make it even more difficult for librarians to feel justified in ordering relevant and representative books. Given the Rees farce, and the recent decision by a theatre company not to embark upon a production of Wilde's *The Importance of Being Earnest* for fear of breaking the law (!), it is perhaps not unreasonable to suggest that one of the more immediate results of Section 28 will be the 'streamlining' of some libraries' already inadequate existing resources. (In 1986, eighteen months *before* the Section had come into effect, an English teacher in a London secondary school requested that the library stock 7 books – from a choice of a possible 160 – from the then recently published *Positive Images*: Materiography no. 11. He was subsequently told by the librarian that the ILEA Libraries Inspectorate 'had withdrawn the *Positive Images* resources'. This turned out to be completely untrue. One of the books which the librarian had refused to stock, even though it had been missed off the resource list, was *Maurice*.

The purpose of this chapter has been to discuss the role of the English department in the introduction of sexuality into the curriculum and what it is that makes it so amenable to the adoption of such a role. Through looking at what English is and how it is perceived by students, as well as how it has already been used as a vehicle for other sociological initiatives, I have argued that English has a vital, possibly even a primary, place in this area. Chapter 4 concentrates on particular strategies and approaches which might be utilized to maximize the contribution which English undoubtedly has to make.

4 Possible strategies

Having described the need for the issue of sexuality to be aired in schools and its appropriateness to the English curriculum, I shall now discuss possible ways in which this might best be achieved. Chapters 5 and 6 will present two case studies for use with upper school secondary students. Both units of work are literature based, each involving a novel written specifically for teenagers: *Who Lies Inside* by Timothy Ireland and *Annie on my Mind* by Nancy Garden.

This chapter seeks to examine some possible methods of integrating the issue of sexuality into the range of English teaching which already exists. It will focus on both the primary and the secondary sectors, as well as on aspects of further education, particularly A level. Finally, it will include discussions of the potential roles of both Media Studies and Drama because, having regard to the proposals for the national curriculum, each appears poised to lose its independent status and is set to become a part of 'Greater' English.

Primary school work

So, when we talk about challenging heterosexism in primary schools, it invokes a deep-rooted fear that we're asking for lessons in lesbian sex for five-year-olds. The media have a field day with such ideas, while radical politicians are apt to desert us at this point, and lump us in with abortion, VD and other 'sensitive issues' which (unfortunately) 'can't be avoided'.

(Anonymous lesbian mother, 'What do we want from Primary Schools',
Gen, March 1987, quoted in Haringey Education Service 1988: 26)

More than in any other sector of the education system, it is the primary school where the most vituperative and profound disagreement with a policy of defusing homophobia is to be found. If most of those who oppose the challenging of heterosexism are content to use rational argument – tinged with only the most delicate hint of 'Victorian values' – when discussing secondary schools, no such luxury is ever afforded to the consideration of the primary sector. It is surely not far from the truth to say that, in relation to lesbian and gay issues, the primary school has become a rhetorical bloodbath. The virtual hysteria, whipped up by the media, on the discovery in a London teacher's centre (misreported as a primary school) of the book, *Jenny lives with Eric and Martin*, sent far-reaching ripples across a huge surface of political waters (see p. 23). Yet, as the quotation above illustrates, there has never been any intention to discuss the issue seriously. It is invariably presumed that the under-11s are merely to receive indoctrination and gratuitous, graphic descriptions of the practical performance of lesbian and gay sex!

However, there is a real need for the issue to be seen as being every bit as relevant in the primary sector as it is elsewhere. It is estimated that about one-third of all lesbians are mothers and a smaller, but none the less significant proportion of gay men are fathers. For many children, homosexuality is not something new or strange; it is the stuff and substance of their domestic lives and to dismiss this as either outside the range of their experience or beyond their comprehension is naive, unrealistic and often deeply offensive. Even for those students who have been brought up in a heterosexual environment, most will have watched *EastEnders* and other television programmes which have dealt with homosexuality. Furthermore, in today's world of HIV, sensationalist journalism and an increasingly open attitude to the discussion of some aspects of sex and sexuality, it is almost impossible to prevent children from encountering at least some allusion to homosexuality. Its meaning, far from evading them, as many argue, will often be clearly understood. This can be evidenced by the fact that, at a surprisingly young age, children will use the words 'lezzie' and 'poof' as the supreme insult and gradually become aware what each denotes.

> School (especially, but not exclusively, the boys) use the usual terms of abuse associated with gays regularly. Gay abuse is to be found from the first year upward. Not in a specifically sexual sense, although the meaning comes into the abuse as the pupils become more sexually aware, but in a generally negative sense. Anyone who might be a bit slow, or dim, or weak, or ugly, or poorly dressed is liable to be called a poof or queer, etc. So whatever a gay person might really be, these pupils soon learn that it is something definitely not to be.
>
> (Mark Baker 1981, quoted in Warren 1984: 13)

Similarly very young children can often be heard making racist or sexist comments, which may have been derived from an adult carer or from the media. Left unchallenged, these are likely to form a part of the child's own attitudes and remain unquestioned. It is just such a fear which has prompted many primary schools to embrace anti-racist and anti-sexist initiatives. To that end, such schools have begun critically to examine the resources and types of language which they use, as well as the expectations which they have of their students.

Resources

It is apparent to those concerned with anti-racist and anti-sexist initiatives that it is virtually impossible, on the one hand, to strive for non-discriminatory teaching practices while, on the other, still presenting materials and books which perpetuate exactly those myths and stereotypes it sought to neuter. All the book *Jenny lives with Eric and Martin* was ever trying to achieve was to even up the coverage of adult relationships which appear in children's books. It attempted to present the normality of a young girl living with her father and his lover. There is certainly a need for such positive images of lesbians and gay men in fiction for young people but, to be fully effective, authors need to steer clear of transposing such representations into the subject matter of their books. As with the best anti-racist and anti-sexist fiction, the images presented must be incidental to the plot, not central to it. The distinction being drawn here is between books which present a positive image of a particular group in the course of their narrative and those whose specific purpose is to open up an issue for discussion. This latter style surely has little place in a strategy designed to counter heterosexism in primary schools.

It is essential that students are given the opportunity to work with a range of different resources which accurately represent both their own individual experiences and those of the world of which they form a part. There is little need specifically to address the options which are presented, nor will most children wish to. Once they are used to a wide variety of life-styles and cultures in the books they read, it will soon become unnecessary for them to question and discuss each one. The important thing at primary level is that that variety is available.

Attitudes and assumptions

Few educationalists would disagree with the statement that, in respect of emotional and cognitive development, the most formative period in a child's school life is between the ages of 5 and 7. The environment and influences to which the child is subjected are likely to have a deep and lasting effect on her/his future. Attitudes, types of preferred behaviour and assumptions will all be transmitted to the young learner, struggling to make sense of her/his world. What we say, how we say it, the way we act; all will be observed and sifted through, in order to find some kind of pattern or model for that child to adopt. If it becomes obvious that certain kinds of conduct will be rewarded while others are disparaged, the child will quickly learn that the best way to achieve what s/he desires is to produce the conduct most acceptable to the adult then in a position to meet those desires.

If a little boy of 5 notices that his teacher becomes upset with him when he plays in the playhouse, he will be faced with the choice of either exacerbating her/his annoyance or seeking to please, albeit at the expense of his own wishes. Similarly if a teacher always uses the personal pronoun 'he' to describe doctors and 'she' for nurses, children will soon pick up on these assumptions and begin to reflect them in their own talk and behaviour. Further, if it is obvious that girls are not expected to take an active part in practical work and boys are encouraged not to cry, not only will students 'read' the messages behind such expectations, but also some will feel pressurized to modify their conduct accordingly. As was pointed out earlier, challenging heterosexism could quite properly (and, perhaps, *ought* to) be seen as merely an extension of an existing anti-sexist commitment, in that both rely so heavily in exploding gender stereotypes.

In conclusion, whatever the media may have suggested, few would seriously argue that the strategies for challenging heterosexism in the primary school ought to be either as direct and confrontational or as factually based as they need to be in secondary schools. Given that prejudice is underpinned by a theoretical component, which has as its *raison d'être* the struggle to gain and maintain power, it would be far too much to expect most primary school students to be able to deconstruct heterosexism at such an ideological level. Therefore teachers are limited, by the capabilities of their students, merely to the presentation of positive images of lesbians and gay men which are incidental to the main work being done and to ensuring that the attitudes and assumptions which they hold do not inhibit the appropriate personal development of those students.

Secondary school work

> At the heart of the educational process lies the child. No advances in policy, no acquisitions of new equipment have their desired effect unless they are in harmony with the nature of the child.
> (Central Advisory Council for England 1967; reproduced in DES 1989)

This quotation says little more than the argument already propounded in Chapter 3, regarding the provision of access to the curriculum for all students. If the work set and the expectations held are not in harmony with the nature of the child, then it is obvious that this will provide unnecessary difficulties for that student. Currently 10 per cent of those whom we teach are being placed in that position.

However, the integration of anti-homophobic practices into the classroom is not intended solely to benefit those students who already identify themselves as lesbian and gay, or even those who will subsequently come to do so. Many students will have a lesbian or gay carer, most will also have lesbian or gay friends (whether they know it or not) and, of those who later become parents themselves, a sizeable minority will produce a lesbian or gay child. Even for those who fall outside the above groups, *all* students are part of a society in which 10 per cent of the population are lesbian and gay. However directly or indirectly the issue affects them, it definitely does affect them. It is a part of their world.

Given that even the national curriculum document, *English for Ages 5 to 16*, views the basis of English as consisting of the four language modes of reading, writing, speaking and listening (DES 1989: para 2.13), I shall examine the possible strategies which are available for each. I have not distinguished between upper and lower school work as, all too often, such a distinction has resulted in the more radical of curricular developments being consigned to lower school classes where the concentration on exam material is less pressing. However, when testing at 7, 11, 14 and 16 is introduced, *all* classes will be potential exam groups. Also, wherever relevant, reference has been made to the proposals for English in the national curriculum, as anything which is suggested hereunder needs to accord (or, at least, not directly conflict) with these.

Reading

> Literature helps secondary pupils to explore and express their own thoughts and feelings and moral and social values and provides a stimulus for discussion with their peers and adults.
>
> (DES 1989: para 3.11)
>
> The books chosen for study should also encompass a balanced range of presentations of other societies, and of ethnic social groupings and *life-styles* within our own society.
>
> (DES 1989: para 11.7, my emphasis)

Nowadays, with the more child-centred direction which contemporary English teaching has taken and the opportunities available with the introduction of more progressive syllabuses for both the language and literature GCSE exams, many departments are able to make use of literature in radically different ways from their precursors. The days of reading a book solely because it is part of some Leavisite canon of great literature are (thankfully) coming to an end. Instead, novels, plays and poetry are increasingly brought into the classroom because they reflect the experiences of students or will be enjoyed by a particular class or because they raise interesting, relevant and/or topical issues. To this end, most schools have now begun the process of balancing up the materials which they use, to reflect better the achievements and importance of women and ethnic minorities within society. Novels such as *The Turbulent Term of Tyke Tyler* (Gene Kemp), *The Basketball Game* (Julius Lester) and *Sumitra's Story* (Rukshana Smith) now regularly take their place alongside more 'mainstream' children's books used in schools. Yet each of these three novels was written specifically to raise a particular issue, albeit within the framework of a conventional narrative for young people.

As the first quotation from the proposals for the national curriculum suggests, the study of literature is an excellent means of accessing both students' own thoughts and feelings, as well as looking at wider moral and social values. The presentation of different narratives allows students to 'experience' a range of situations and individual's responses to them; situations and responses which they might not necessarily come across in their everyday lives. This provides students with the opportunity to discuss the most intimate thoughts and emotions of a character in what is a totally depersonalized context.

The past few years has seen a flurry of novels written for adolescents on the subject of homosexuality. Most of these are about young gay men, but there is a growing catalogue of fiction which deals sympathetically with the lives of young lesbians. The major benefit of raising issues of homosexuality through a novel is that the intimate thoughts and emotions of a lesbian or gay person can be presented and discussed without a real person risking the possibility of any kind of negative responses. Most of these novels, many of which are extremely well-written, appear to be appropriate for students aged 14 and over.

No doubt, due to the primacy accorded to emotion and self-expression in the genre as a whole, there is a large amount of lesbian and gay-related poetry available. Little has been written specifically for students but, none the less, there is much within mainstream, adult collections and anthologies which can be used. Poetry is a particularly useful medium through which to introduce concepts of sexuality, given that its essence rests upon suggestion rather than statement, allowing students to interpret rather than receive meaning directly.

There appear to be fewer suitable plays, dealing sensitively with lesbian and gay issues. True, there have been a number of recent productions relating to HIV/AIDS and gay men, but it would seem to be of little real benefit to concentrate on the one aspect of gay male experience which has been so publicized, as to push its importance well beyond the point of distortion. (A selection of suitable novels, short stories, poetry and plays can be found in the resource list in the appendix.)

Writing

Pupils should have opportunities to write for a wider range of communicative or informative purposes, including: describing, explaining, giving instructions, reporting, expressing a point of view, persuading, comparing and contrasting ideas, arguing for different points of view. They should have increasing opportunities to use writing for private purposes, such as reviewing their own experiences, reflecting on their own ideas and formulating hypotheses.

(DES 1989: para 17.54)

As was seen in Chapter 3, a sizeable proportion of the writing which English teachers currently set requires students to draw on their own personal experience and present their own ideas. Looking at the proposals relating to writing, if anything, this dependency is to be increased. In the quotation above, students are to be given opportunities for 'expressing a point of view, persuading, comparing and contrasting ideas, arguing for different points of view', as well as 'reviewing their own experiences, reflecting on their own ideas and formulating hypotheses.' The first four of these modes fall, broadly, within what teachers have come to call discursive writing, the staple of most English syllabuses for 14–16-year-olds in the UK. In many ways, it is one of the most difficult skills in which students can achieve anything more than competence. Dealing with abstractions, as it does, it requires students to stand back from a particular debate and balance conflicting theories and ideas objectively, before being in a position to reach a conclusion and express their own views. Too often the subject matter, albeit contentious, is insufficient to engage them to the point of being able to achieve the necessary distance and then be able to argue in a dispassionate way.

This leads to the other three modes for writing, isolated by the national curriculum document; those of 'reviewing their own experiences, reflecting on their own ideas and formulating hypotheses.' The same document rightly points out that 'the best writing is vigorous, *committed, honest* and interesting' (DES 1989: para 17.31, my emphasis). Issues such as capital punishment, nuclear weapons and/or power, equality between the sexes, vivisection, and whether George (in *Of Mice and Men*) was a hero, often fail to provide students with that spark which is needed to kindle good discursive writing. (Which of *us* would feel motivated to produce, for instance, a newspaper column on an issue in which we had little more than a passing interest?)

Sexuality, however, is an area which is of relevance and of interest to all students, irrespective of their current or future orientation. As young people begin to carve out their own niche in the world in which they find themselves, sexuality, how it is that they identify themselves as emotional and sexual beings, takes on a central role in that process. It is for just this reason that the discussion of issues of sex-stereotyping is such an important part of anti-sexist practice. To harness this pre-existent interest to English work can result only in writing which is more committed, whether the piece is written from a personal or an 'objective' standpoint.

As can be seen in the case studies in Chapters 5 and 6, writing produced in the role of a particular fictional character can provide excellent opportunities for students to confront issues which they would normally shun if speaking with their own voice. On a more abstract level, a response to a text which touches upon lesbian or gay themes will still require them to contemplate these themes, but with the provision of an even greater distance between themselves and the subject matter.

Perhaps of the four language modes, it is writing which provides the widest range of possibilities for teachers concerned with the integration of anti-homophobic work in their current practices. As a result of its being a predominantly personal task, it is easier to neutralize the potency of peer pressure than is the case with oral work. In addition to this, students are already used to writing in role. Diaries, newspaper articles, letters, all currently constitute a major part of our teaching. All that the teacher, committed to combating heterosexism, needs to do is to alter their content, through the use of a range of different stimuli.

Speaking and listening

Even the world's most prolific writers will speak and listen far more than they will ever write. However many books are on our shelves, we will have spoken and heard millions more words than we have ever read. As young children, we learn to make sense of our world through asking questions. It is from talking and listening that we learn language. In our society, someone who can interact with other people but can neither read nor write is seen as being no more than linguistically disadvantaged and might be encouraged to attend adult literacy classes. Yet someone who spends their whole life reading but is incapable of normal social intercourse with others is deemed to have a personality disorder and would be referred for psychiatric or psychoanalytic help. In everyday life, talking and listening far supersede reading and writing in both their pervasiveness and their importance. But it is only in the last few years that oracy has taken its place alongside literacy as a valid part of schools' English curricula. Even now, due to the difficulties inherent in its assessment, most exam boards tend to tag the oral component on to the end of the (main) written grade. The spoken word is, after all, a very different animal compared to its written cousin.

> The structure and patterns of spoken language are distinct from those of writing: it is rare, for example, for a speaker continuously to use complete sentences as we understand them in writing – particularly in a situation where interruption is both accepted and expected. Similarly, oral language differs significantly from written language in its complex interactive nature: non-verbal communication, such as body language is also a part of the process.
>
> (DES 1989: para 15.14)

By the time they arrive at secondary school, whatever learning difficulties they may otherwise have, most English-as-first-language students will be relatively effective oral communicators. In the sphere of social communication, they are already highly socialized and interactive and there is comparatively little that they need to learn from teachers which they won't pick up through their everyday talk with friends and family. However, one area in which students may need help is structured, transactional talk. To this end, teachers of English have become skilled in the provision of opportunities for pair, group and whole-class work although, again, the majority of these still seem limited to the lower school.

Role-play, problem-solving and discussion work are all, obviously, highly amenable to encompassing a wide variety of different subject matter. In fact, it could be argued that it is invariably the form which is more important than the content. After all, it is the skills of varied communication in which we seek to give students practice and the way we achieve this is surely incidental. To an extent this is true, but, as is the case with writing, if students are not committed to the work which they are doing, it is unlikely that they will produce much that is of any great value.

Again, given the pre-existent interest in aspects of sexuality and its 'contentious' nature, it would seem to be tailor-made for oral tasks. Many of the activities in the two case studies in Chapters 5 and 6 rely on oral work and are included because they provide students with the opportunity to make instant responses to what they are doing within each unit. As with the suggestions for writing, we need do little more than alter its content in order to make use of oral work as an effective part of any strategy to defuse homophobia.

Further education

I shall focus upon A level English, albeit that many students have the opportunity to continue their studies at school rather than at a college of further education. For those courses like re-sits, Communications or those which contain an English component as part of their overall assessment, it may well be more useful, given the type of work required, to refer back to what has been said in relation to secondary school English.

Despite the radical changes in the UK which have occurred over the past fifteen years in exams at 16, the A level syllabus has remained virtually intact, concerning itself almost totally with literature. While GCSE has forced the 'Classics' to make way for texts perceived as more child-centred and has blurred, if not completely obliterated, the old distinction between GCE and CSE, little has really altered at 16+. True, there is now the opportunity to include some coursework, as well as texts which students have selected and exam boards have, at least, nodded in the direction of Black and Asian writers. But the basic content has not altered substantively. By the time students begin 16+ education, it is surely fairly difficult to maintain the argument that they are still somehow too young or immature to understand and cope with the concept of homosexuality. It is at around this age when relationships and sex take on a primacy in many of their lives. Much of their time will be spent in contemplating the adult world and their own place within it. To this end, they will analyse a wide range of stimuli as potential role models. It is therefore essential that they receive as comprehensive a variety of modes of behaviour and attitude as is possible.

It is perhaps in the sphere of literature, the major component of most A level syllabuses, where the issue of sexuality is most pertinent. This is not just on the basis of the arguments made in relation to reading and the secondary school. For reasons which are outside the scope of this book, a disproportionate number of the authors whose works appear on A level syllabuses were either lesbian or gay. Often this may not be of particular textual relevance, as with, for example, much of Marlowe, but it is surely short-sighted in the extreme to fail to raise it when reading Forster's *Maurice*, much of the poetry of Auden and almost all that of Whitman, as well as some of the works of Katherine Mansfield and, of course, anything at all by Wilde. It is also worth remembering that the vast majority of Shakespeare's sonnets were inspired by and written for 'Mr W H', whose identity, but not gender, is still the subject of fierce academic controversy.

> The sins of omission (ignoring the sexuality of literary figures) destroy legitimate cultural recognition of alternative modes of living and loving, perpetuating cultural lies and misleading literary interpretations.
>
> (Follett 1982)

This failure to inform students of the sexuality of authors whose works they study has a number of consequences. First, some texts will be difficult to appreciate if the motivating force behind their production is ignored. *The Importance of Being*

Earnest will actually evade full comprehension if Wilde's homosexuality and the codes he used in the text partially to disguise references to it are not explored. Second, failing to know an author's sexuality deprives *all* students of contact with and knowledge about influential and famous lesbians and gay men, compounding the myth that the only well-known homosexual is the one who is notorious. Third, it denies lesbian and gay students access to potentially successful and helpful role models. Fourth, as a direct result of this, they are unable to develop feelings of pride in the culture of which they form a part. Finally, this apparent invisibility of lesbians and gay men in literature (as in almost every sphere of human achievement) can only increase the pressure on students to maintain their own invisibility and strengthen the belief that their experiences and emotions are neither expressed nor fit into the dominant culture.

It is surely untenable, given the sheer number of texts with lesbian and gay themes which are either prescribed or deemed admissible by current syllabuses, for teachers of A level not to highlight the importance of sexuality in the literature which they choose. The opportunities exist, not only because such texts are to be studied, but also because a failure to do so may result in clouding rather than explaining the work.

Media Studies

> Media education . . . seeks to increase children's critical understanding of the media – namely, television, film, video, radio, photography, popular music, printed materials, and computer software. How they work, how they produce meaning, how they are organised and how audiences make sense of them, are the issues that media education addresses. [It] aims to develop systematically children's critical and creative powers through analysis and production of media artefacts. This also deepens their understanding of the pleasure and enjoyment provided by the media. Media education aims to create more active and more critical media users who will demand, and could contribute to, a greater range of diversity of media products.
>
> (Bazalgette 1989, reprinted in DES 1989: paras. 9–6)

Few would seek to argue substantially with Bazalgette's excellent definition of media education. In order to transform such worthy aims into practice, as an example, the 1990 LEAG syllabus for GCSE Media Studies isolates four key concepts which the exam board see as forming the core of a Media Studies course: *forms and conventions, representation, media institutions* and *audience.* At a pedagogic level, these require that students achieve competence in three main areas. First, they need to gain a clear understanding of how it is that media companies actually work. Second, they have to acquire the skills of analysing and comparing different media products. Third, it is essential that students gain practical skills so as to allow them to create and produce media materials of their own.

Interpreting this course outline, it soon becomes clear that Media Studies provides the teacher with a large number of opportunities to raise the issue of sexuality. The concept of *representation*, who and what is presented and how and why those images are chosen, is an ideal vehicle to examine how the mainstream media decide to represent particular groups within society. Invariably this will require some analysis of bias and power. For this reason, teachers have often concentrated on the place of women or ethnic minorities, but it is equally possible to integrate issues relating to the representation of lesbians and gay men.

In respect of *media institutions*, students will need to look at who has access to the production processes of different media, how the institutions themselves are controlled and financed and how their 'excesses' can be curbed. Again, it is appropriate, and often will be essential, to examine the role of minority groups, including lesbians and gay men, in these processes.

Similarly the concept of *audience* can provide a useful forum for combating heterosexism. Some 10 per cent of media consumers are likely to be lesbian or gay. It might well be instructive to pay attention to how different media choose to address this particular audience on a general level and how they try (if they ever do) to target it specifically. This could lead to an examination of what comeback both individuals and groups have if they feel that they have been misrepresented or ignored. Alternative and minority media can be considered to see if and how they rectify this imbalance.

Drama

The purpose of drama education is to develop the powers of the mind so that a 'common' understanding of life can be mastered. Common understanding cuts across the 'forms' of knowledge and is a rigorous way of approaching school subjects from the 'inside', rather than from the more normal view of a subject as a collection of 'given' knowledge.

(Bolton 1984:89)

The contemporary view of drama in education, as espoused by Bolton, is as a technique for acquiring knowledge and experience through the tools of simulation, role-play and dramatic activity. This 'acquisition' has been defined by Dorothy Heathcote (in Bolton 1984:167) as the search to find 'the universal at the centre of the particular'. She argues that it is not solely the intention of drama to place students in the role of a particular character, at a particular time. It seeks, instead, to allow students to glimpse the universality of all those who have been in that position.

[Drama in education] is seen as a vehicle for cognitive development giving significance to the learning of those kinds of concepts which, while cutting across the traditional subject barriers, are nevertheless of central importance to living.

(Bolton 1986:245–6)

This quotation attempts to provide the *raison d'être* for the use of drama in schools. It argues that drama allows students to become acquainted with concepts essential for life. These fall into two categories. First, there are the 'process' skills which will be acquired as a result of engaging in drama: those skills which are intrinsic to group work, of trust and co-operation. Second, there is the substantive content of the drama itself: this relates to the negotiation of meaning which is inherent in the activities undertaken. It is here that Heathcote's quest for the universal comes into its own.

In terms of content, drama has often been seen, in Heathcote's words, as about 'A man [sic] in a mess'. Despite the statement's simplicity and the tendency for it to have been interpreted as an almost exclusive concentration on locating suitable crises and then focusing upon them rather than their effects in human terms, similar pithy catch-phrases, albeit more clearly 'framed' in terms of personal empathy, still pervade theories of contemporary drama. As a working definition, 'drama as the resolution of a problem' is perhaps as useful as any.

If these definitions and formulae are accepted, it then becomes clear that drama is an ideal medium through which to raise issues pertinent to sexuality. It is for this very reason that so much drama already focuses on prejudice. Its concentration on problem-solving, through empathetic role-play and response, would appear to be ideal for an examination of oppression. But, as elsewhere in the curriculum, this is invariably limited to aspects of race, sex and, occasionally, class.

A situation which involves a child coming out to her/his carers or where a group of students is victimizing an individual due to their belief in her/his homosexuality are merely two of the possible contexts which would be amenable for use in drama. In one London school, the Section 28 debate was effectively used with a GCSE drama group as a springboard from which to examine issues of personal freedom and repression.

All that is being argued is that teachers of drama embrace the contextual possibilities which are brought out by raising the issue of sexuality and utilize them within their pre-existing curricular framework. None of the pedagogical aims or objectives of drama would require modification, yet its focus, so important to Heathcote, would be widened to include more occasions to awaken students to the universal at the centre of the particular.

The purpose, then, of this chapter has been to examine the possible strategies which could be adopted in order to integrate issues of sexuality into the pre-existent English curriculum. This has been attempted on the basis of the four language modes, as well as both Media Studies and Drama and, wherever appropriate, reference has been made to the document, *The National Curriculum: English for Ages 5 to 16* (DES 1989). It is hoped that it has been demonstrated that it is perfectly possible to achieve a more realistic and equitable treatment of lesbian and gay issues within the rubric of existing practices and, perhaps more importantly, as part of the national curriculum when it is fully implemented.

5

Case study 1: *Who Lies Inside* by Timothy Ireland

The schemes of work which follow in this and the next chapter are intended for use with a class of between twenty and twenty-five mixed-ability 15–16-year-old students, although, of course, each could be modified according to specific needs. They ought to be equally suitable with mixed-sex groups, but it might be felt that, in a single-sex environment, Case Study 1 is more appropriate with young men, while Case Study 2 would work better with young women. Each assumes that students have previously examined issues of anti-racism and anti-sexism and, consequently, are relatively well versed in the discourse of prejudice. It is envisaged that in the UK the work produced as a result of these units will form a part of the students' language and/or literature (or dual certification) GCSE coursework folder.

The aim of both is to present some concrete ideas for the teacher of English, anxious to do 'something' in an attempt to combat homophobia. Doubtless, each has drawbacks: there are some scenes which might be deemed to be too explicit (although not impossible) to discuss with some classes. However, their major strength lies in that, as literature-based courses, they remove the subject from the realm of the teacher's hobby-horse and place it within the context of set books, whose themes and issues are to be explored as part of students' GCSE coursework. None the less, as with all the resources suggested throughout this book, attention needs to be paid to the arguments made in Chapter 7, which deals with 'precautions' which teachers might want to take to stop their usage backfiring on them.

It is important to re-emphasize here that, as with good anti-sexist and anti-racist teaching, a half-term's work on its own will do little but act as a sop to the conscience. Anti-oppressive education *must* pervade the entire curriculum constantly. That does not mean that it must always be mentioned and taught: far from it. Forming an integral part of the school curriculum, the countering of prejudice will *inform* rather than *lead* the curriculum. It will become one of the many yardsticks by which the content of courses will be measured. Equally, both case studies require that the teacher is well informed as to some of the more complex issues which each raises and has taken the time to research those areas which are outside individual personal experience and knowledge. None the less, it is intended that the materials included here will allow the issue of sexuality to gain a foothold on an English curriculum where the spirit might be willing, but the body is tied up with a thousand and one other tasks, such as profiling.

Outline and plot synopsis

The novel I have chosen around which to base this first course of work is *Who Lies Inside* by Timothy Ireland (first published in 1984 by Gay Men's Press); it has already been used by at least two London schools as a GCSE text.

Martin Conway is a sixth-former, who describes himself as someone you might see 'on any street in any town'. He plays rugby, goes out drinking with his mates and is studying for his A levels. However, he has just become aware that he is gay. The story charts the impact of this discovery upon Martin and those around him. It is a well-written book yet is still appropriate across the range of ability and linguistic competence usually found in 15–16-year-olds. It is an intensely moving story which treats its subject matter with much sensitivity; guilty neither of syrupy sentimentality, nor of degenerating into graphic sexual description. The title is the question which Martin continually asks himself, but the real power of the novel lies in the fact that this is the question which is relevant to all the book's characters and to the readers themselves. Beneath the roles which each of us is conditioned to adopt by society lies our 'real self'. Due to the universality of the question, Ireland need not rely on portraying Martin as a victim; the 'stranger' beneath his skin is merely that part of him which has been buried and which he ultimately comes to know.

What follows is an annotated schema of lessons which has as its central theme *Who Lies Inside*. The complete unit is intended to run for a period of a six-week half-term. It is based on several assumptions, deviation from which ought not to be problematic. These include the timetabled provision for three seventy-minute lessons and one substantial piece of homework per week. A class set of the novel is available but students are not able to take them home, so all the reading has to be done in class. (Additional materials mentioned in the scheme are marked with an asterisk* and fuller details can be found at the end of this chapter, pp. 70–4.)

Who Lies Inside: the scheme of work

Week 1 Lesson 1

- Distribute copies of 'You are my good teachers'*. In threes or fours, ask students to work towards a presentation of the poem.
- Select three or four different versions and have them presented.

- Class discussion touching on stereotypes, 'plight' of lesbian or gay student, etc.

The aim of this lesson is merely to introduce the subject in a general way. The poem makes the point that homophobia is a prejudice, no different in 'theory' or practice from either racism or sexism. The discussion should be as little teacher-led as practicable, so as to give students an opportunity to air their views openly. Care should be taken to ensure that the discussion never becomes too personal. Although they will come as no great surprise, the different strands of prejudice which are likely to be exhibited should be noted down so that they can be 'answered' in due course. The main purpose of the lesson is just to open up the subject.

Week 1 Lesson 2

- Hand out novel. Read Chapter 1 (pp. 7–23).
- Give students the extract from *The Naked Civil Servant* by Quentin Crisp* (pp. 66–8), where the author is set upon in the street. In pairs, ask them to dramatize this; not for whole class performance. Ensure that all swap roles from victim to aggressor.
- Set written work: Charles's diary entry for the evening he is beaten up in the Roebuck, to be started in any remaining time in the lesson and completed at home, ready to hand in on Week 2 Lesson 1.

Chapter 1 tells of Martin's first realization of his sexuality, his relationship with his best friend, Steve, and of an incident in a local pub in which Charles, an 'obviously' gay man, is beaten up and the effect which this has upon Martin. It is a powerful start and might benefit from the comparison with Crisp's autobiography. The swapping of parts in the role-play ought to involve some empathetic responses which should inform and be reinforced in the diary writing.

Week 1 Lesson 3

- Hand out one piece of sugar paper and one marker pen to each group of four or five students. Ask them to write 'Rugby Player' in the centre of the paper and to encircle it. They are then to complete the spidergram with as many words brought to mind by 'Rugby Player' as they can.
- Draw replica spidergram on the board completing it with suggestions. Ask if these are 'right' or helpful. Do these stereotypical assumptions cause harm? Why? And so on.
- Read Chapter 2 (pp. 24–32).

The spidergram and the ensuing discussions ought to highlight the role into which Martin has been forced. It should also reiterate the unhelpfulness of such assumptions in general and prepare the class for the next chapter, in which Martin struggles with his parents, friends and himself in order to retain his 'false' identity, rather than unleash the 'stranger'. This is made all the more difficult by his shared glances and day-to-day contact with Richard, a fellow student, to whom he is increasingly attracted.

Week 2 Lesson 1

- Collect Charles's diary.
- Give brief résumé of plight of lesbians and gay men at the hands of the Nazis. Use extracts from *The Men with the Pink Triangles* by Heinz Heger* (pp. 33, 34): arrival at Sachsenhausen, etc.
- Read Chapter 3 (pp. 33–51).
- Play a recording of 'Smalltown Boy' by Bronski Beat. Ask class to write down initial impressions of its meaning. Hand out the lyrics* and get them to write the story behind them, which can be handed in in the following lesson.

This is likely to be the most difficult lesson within this unit. Chapter 3 contains descriptions of Martin's embarrassment when sharing a shower with Steve, memories of their innocent, erotic and exploratory play when they were both 13 and Martin's growing desire for Richard. To ameliorate the adverse reactions which students may well have to this and to provide the necessary background to the excesses of homophobia, I suggest first giving a brief history of the Nazi persecution of lesbians and gay men and then using a small extract from Heger's account of experiences of gay inmates in concentration camps. It is both a shocking and a nauseating study in deprivation; yet, historically and practically, it appears to be essential that students know about what happened to the 100 000 men and women, who all too often disappear from any catalogue of Hitler's victims. If they are not exposed to the truth of what took place, it will be that much more difficult for them adequately to confront their own prejudices and be ready to respond sensitively to stories such as Martin's.

The Bronski Beat record deals with the fate of a young gay man who is forced to leave his home town, after he is beaten up by a man whom he has been eyeing up. His parents are unable either to accept his sexuality or to help him, so he packs his bags and sets off for 'the bright lights'. Although a hit in 1984, it is still an extremely popular record and one students will know. This makes it an ideal resource when looking for material suitable for empathetic writing.

Week 2 Lesson 2

- Collect 'Smalltown Boy' homework.
- Assemble wide selection of love poetry across the whole emotional spectrum, ensuring that there are several poems for each student. Arrange them on a desk in the centre of the room, having cleared away the remaining furniture. Invite students to read poems either to themselves or each other and to select their favourite(s). The teacher should be available to read 'requests'.
- Read Chapter 4 (pp. 52–60).

The purpose of this lesson is to try to blur the distinctions between lesbian and gay and heterosexual relationships and instead concentrate on the range of emotions and behaviour which they share. Chapter 4 is concerned solely with Martin's visit to Richard's house and the fear and awkwardness which he feels. This needs to be viewed within a context which is recognizable to the students and it is hoped an 'immersion' in love poetry ought to make them more receptive to this. On an individual level, the teacher should try to engage students in informal conversation about experiences of their own personal relationships which they want to share, focusing, where possible, on any instances where they themselves have felt embarrassment or a lack of self-confidence.

Week 2 Lesson 3

- Work on the *Capital Gay* article, dealing with police raid on Vauxhall Tavern*.
- Work in groups of four or five on a video to accompany 'Smalltown Boy' to be filmed next week.

The newspaper article, which appeared as the lead story in the London newspaper *Capital Gay* on 30 January 1987, describes a police raid on the Vauxhall Tavern, a well-known gay pub in South London. It was a 'routine' drugs raid but, in the event, the police uncovered only amyl nitrate, commonly known as 'poppers', a vaporous substance used to heighten sexual excitement. It is not currently illegal in the UK. The main point of the story, however, is that many of the officers arrived wearing surgical gloves. The article is included to demonstrate first, the widespread stereotyping of *all* gay men as AIDS carriers, and second, the levels of ignorance which exist as far as HIV infection is concerned.

The video task is designed to extend the empathetic work begun the preceding week. Students will need to take on the role of young lesbians or gay men, forced to leave home due to violence and victimization offered in direct response to their sexuality. Although this is, without a doubt, an extremely difficult thing to ask them to do, it is hoped that the promise of producing a pop video will serve as some form of carrot! 'Smalltown Boy' is intended to bridge the gap between those facets of homosexuality which are within their experience and those which are, on the whole, alien to them. However, it is worth remembering here, as elsewhere, that at least 10 per cent of the class may have a clearer understanding of these issues than might the teacher.

Week 3 Lesson 1

- Read Chapters 5 and 6 (pp. 61–82).
- Continue group work on 'Smalltown Boy' video, to be ready for presentation/ filming later in the week.

Both of these short chapters contain little action but focus upon the growing chasm opening up between Martin and those to whom he has been close. He has important and provocative conversations with his friend, Linda, and his parents (Chapter 5) and Tom (the rugby trainer) and Charles (Chapter 6). Finally, out of a sense of desperation, he phones Linda late one night and confesses his love for Richard. He then hangs up. Despite their lack of action, these two chapters are essential in the portrayal of the struggle which Martin experiences and the sense of isolation he feels. This seems to be ideal, relevant input for students while they are involved in the preparation of their videos. Martin's plight is exemplified in that there is no one to whom he can talk or share his feelings and this ultimately drives him into a totally irrational and badly timed disclosure, rather than bottling up his secret any longer.

Week 3 Lesson 2

- Last-minute rehearsal of videos.
- Recording of individual groups, preferably in a separate room.
- Those yet to be filmed, or whose work has already been filmed, can begin to design a booklet on aspects of sexuality, to be used by 13–14-year-old students during work on sex education. This is to be a continuing piece of work and specific areas and types of information to be included ought to be made clear.

It should be possible to record five four-minute videos in the space of one lesson. This might require the presence of another member of staff to supervise the filming and to ensure that time limits are respected. The booklet is intended to provide students with an opportunity, in the context of an impersonal piece of extended writing, both to assess and to extend their knowledge and thoughts on sexuality and sex-stereotyping. As it is to be an informative (and therefore neutral) guide, there should be little external pressure on them to be abusive about or fight shy of the issue, afraid that what they write will be taken as some form of personal statement. By the end of this unit of work, they ought to have a clear and concise exposition of information relating to homosexuality. These booklets might then form a valuable resource for current and subsequent 13–14-year-old students.

Week 3 Lesson 3

- Read Chapter 7 (pp. 83–9).
- Show the five videos.
- Show the 'original' Bronski Beat video.
- Class discussion arising from the critical viewing of the videos and developing into an examination of isolation and misunderstanding: the 'it's a phase' argument.
- Set homework, which is to continue with the booklets.

Chapter 7 deals with the first meeting of Martin and Linda since Martin's desperate phone call. She is sympathetic, but hopes it is merely a phase, which the love of a good woman will sort out. Martin then plays squash with Steve, who has obviously been told by Linda, because their game is conducted in complete silence and, later, in the changing-room, Steve is clearly embarrassed by his nakedness. By the close of the chapter, Martin is so miserable that he is contemplating suicide. This is clearly a good time to show and discuss the students' videos, first, because of the obvious correlation between the subject matter of both the novel and the video, and second, the ensuing discussion ought to provide them with the chance to articulate and modify their thoughts and emotions regarding Martin's plight as a result of their own work. It is vital that they appreciate that the only person to whom he can talk, Linda, refuses to accept the substance of what he says and instead minimizes it by suggesting that it's only a phase which he will grow out of. Not only that, but also she breaches a confidence. This lack of any empathetic outlet is one of the central themes in both the novel and any discussion of homosexuality itself. Until people realize the isolation and misery which their intolerance and erroneous theorizing cause, there can be little hope of improvement in the quality of life for lesbian and gay students. If it is possible to obtain (and there is sufficient time), it might also be useful to show the 'original' video which was produced to accompany the record when it was released.

Week 4 Lesson 1

- Read 'The cutting room'*.
- Ask students, with as little conferring as possible, to 'brainstorm' a list of words suggested by the word 'lesbian'.
- Amalgamate these into a list on the board. Question the inclusion of each as it is offered, trying to achieve a consensus on a list of five words.
- In groups of five, get students to discuss and write a logical justification of one of the words from the list.
- Hear a report back from each group and through discussion and a vote, see how many of the words 'survive'.

This lesson is intended to bring to the fore a consideration of lesbians, invisible in the novel. I think it is vital that the two 'kinds' of homosexuality are viewed as having much in common; as same-sex relationships, in the prejudice engendered by each and as alternative life-styles. However, it is important not to fall into the trap of oversimplification, presenting lesbians merely as female gay men. 'The cutting room' is a short story about three women who work in the pathology department of a gynaecology clinic. One, Kelly, is a lesbian and the story tells of the misery and discomfort she experiences having to feign heterosexuality. Forced to sit in silence, while Brenda and Josie speculate as to the sexuality of their colleagues and mutual acquaintances, she is frightened to enlighten them. Although both the language and the imagery of the story are complex, it provides a good 'way in' to an initial understanding of lesbian experience. The other activities in this session are designed to demonstrate the unhelpfulness of labelling. In requiring students to produce justifications for their generalizations, the point ought to be made that not only is stereotyping inaccurate, but also it is misleading.

Week 4 Lesson 2

- Screening of video, *True Romance, Etc.*.
- In same-sex friendship pairs, ask students to improvise a role-play. The only instruction should be that their scene involves two friends having a conversation about homosexuality at a party. They need to retain brief, written notes of the dialogue produced.

The video deals with issues of sexism and sexuality through the medium of a story based around an all-night party. This is interspersed with snippets of young lesbians and gay men talking about their lives and experiences. It is an extremely accessible film, not only informative and entertaining, but also (almost uniquely) one which presents positive images of white and Black lesbians and gay men. The subsequent role-play is intended to explore further these positive aspects. Class discussion, were it to take place here, carries the risk that students would focus upon lesbians and gay men as either victims or outsiders, for whom sexuality is a problem and life miserable. However, the role-play, whose subject matter has been left deliberately vague, ought to provide the right opportunity in which they can examine the more positive facets of homosexuality in the relatively unpressured and informal context of working with a friend of the same sex.

Week 4 Lesson 3

- Continue role-play, stipulating a time limit of, say, twenty minutes.
- Ask pairs to write a short play, based on their dialogue, which again would be suitable for use with groups of 13–14-year-old students, to be started in the lesson and finished at home. It is therefore essential that notes are made.
- Re-read the last two pages of Chapter 7 (pp. 88–9) of *Who Lies Inside* and then continue with Chapter 8 (pp. 90–100).

The first part of the lesson is to enable students to 'recapture' and continue their role-play, subject to a time limit whose intention is to bring about its rapid completion. It is hoped that they will have brought fresh ideas with them, having had time to ruminate on their work since the last lesson. After this they are to start working towards a written draft in the form of a play. This should encourage them to rationalize their ideas and aim to present them coherently, conscious of a prospective audience. (The teacher should try to ensure that by the end of a further ten minutes, each student has a rough idea of the dialogue and knows which section s/he is to work on.) The purpose of re-reading the last few paragraphs of Chapter 7 is to remind the class that when they last left Martin, he was contemplating suicide, over a week ago. This should rekindle interest in the novel and bring back its main events.

Chapter 8 takes up the story some four weeks later. Martin is now going out with a young woman from college called Margaret. Before going out one evening, he brings her home to meet his parents. He is aware that he wants only her friendship, yet on their way home, they kiss and he becomes aroused. Her parents are going away the following weekend and, as the house will be empty, they decide that they will spend the Saturday night together. At school the next day, which is the last before the sixth-form leave for revision, Martin finds himself becoming nostalgic for his youth. Then he sees Richard who, up until then, he has ignored. Although their conversation appears stilted, 'something' passes between them and it is as though each can see what lies inside the other.

Week 5 Lesson 1

- Read Chapter 9 (pp. 101–12).
- Hand out poem '28th September'* and ask students in pairs to read it to one another. Circulate and listen and try to provoke an examination of Martin's conduct.
- Then, working individually, they should write the sort of poem which Margaret might have written after Martin left. These should be collected in at the end.

Chapter 9 deals with the evening when Martin and Margaret sleep together. Before he leaves, Martin is subjected to some more of his father's sexist advice; yet his overwhelming feelings are of disgust and contempt for himself and the hurt he is about to cause. Later when he and Margaret are in a pub, he drinks heavily and ignores her. Back at her house, they have sex but, all the time, Martin is aware only of himself and his own gratification. Immediately afterwards, despite her entreaties, he gets dressed, apologizes and leaves. Next time they play squash, Steve is eager to flatter Martin's new-found 'masculinity', by seeking to compare notes and giving him advice as to how best to treat women. At the end of the chapter, Martin's eleventh-hour revision is interrupted, first, by a rare moment of tenderness with his mother and, then, by the arrival of a Good Luck card from Richard.

Although Martin is clearly ashamed of his behaviour before, during and after the act, it is important that students are made fully aware of the unpleasant and sexist way he treats Margaret, from her point of view. To this end, I have suggested using the poem, '28th September', which is about sex 'had' for its own sake. With careful hints and suggestions from the teacher, it ought to be possible to facilitate some highly valuable empathetic talk about the way Margaret must feel. This should be consolidated in the individual poetry work, in which students are to produce the kind of poem which she might write after Martin leaves.

Week 5 Lesson 2

- Final preparation and rehearsal of 'party' plays, whose scripts were to have been completed at home. (See Week 4 Lesson 3)
- Divide class into two, so that there are two same-sex groups of approximately six pairs. Each pair is to perform their play to the rest of their group. (Again it is useful, if possible, to have the assistance of another teacher who can work with one of the groups in another room.)
- Whole class reactions and discussion of individual plays and what they think has been learnt as a result.

The practical difficulties involved with this lesson may well mean that it will have to be modified. The rationale for suggesting same-sex groups and an additional teacher, preferably of the opposite gender to the teacher's own, is two-fold. First, a performance by each pair, in front of the whole class, would result in an apparently long and boring lesson. Second, there is a large risk of embarrassing or silencing some students, by asking them to present their work before too large (and potentially hostile) a group. It should be borne in mind that these are still fairly early days as far as students' exposure to a serious discussion of the subject of homosexuality is concerned and, for this reason, it seems to be vital to opt for same-sex groups, if at all possible, rather than risk any useful work which has been done. It is hoped that if this unit has had any success in altering students' perceptions of homosexuality, the subject matter of the plays will be of a fairly personal nature, as between women and women and men and men. Therefore to subject students, at this juncture, to a mixed-sex audience might well create problems and jeopardize much of what has been learnt. One can hope only that the opportunities for valuable interaction which have been lost, through the need for segregation, will be partially compensated for in the plenary session at the end of the lesson.

Week 5 Lesson 3

- Return marked poems and ask students to produce final drafts, which are to go into a group anthology.
- Set up five 'pressure groups'. Each is told to organize itself, both as to its aims and each individual's function within the group. Suggestions as to the remit for the groups can be made by the teacher. (Some examples appear below.)

The poetry which the students wrote earlier in the week should have been marked. The marking ought to have focused on providing positive comments and suggesting possible ways of developing the pieces, restricting error correction to only the most unavoidable. Returning to the poems, aware that they are to be published and read by others, it is hoped that students will be mindful of comments made and should produce final drafts of a high standard.

The pressure groups are to serve a dual purpose. First, students ought to be made to appreciate that the issue of homosexuality has a political dimension and that the minimal advances which have been made and which are still sought are only ever realized through the mechanism of political pressure. Second, the sort of information which they will require for a campaign will probably be more detailed than that which they already possess, meaning that each group will need to research new areas and be able to report their findings to the rest of the class. Suggestions for possible work might include: a campaign to provide reliable information on HIV/AIDS for *all* students, a group monitoring the implications of Section 28, a consultation body looking at sex education in schools, a body charged with putting together a booklist on the subject, a group formed to check on heterosexism within the school, and so on.

Week 6 Lesson 1

• Read Chapter 10 (pp. 110–27).
• Discussion of whether it is a happy ending? What might happen next? Who did lie inside? And so on.
• Return to pressure groups, aiming to present plans of attack by Week 6 Lesson 3.
• Set up homework: 400-word book review of *Who Lies Inside*.

The final chapter deals with the time after the exams have finished. At the school dance, Martin is unable even to be civil to Margaret and instead seeks solitude in the garden. Once there, he encounters Richard. The latter is initially cool towards him, having been ignored for weeks, but gradually conversation develops and becomes more friendly. Eventually Martin explains how scared he has been. Richard says that he has been too. Finally they touch, as if by accident. They kiss. At this point, Linda comes into the garden, but not before they have arranged to spend the following day at the seaside. She completely ignores Richard and is short with Martin. Richard then leaves and she and Martin have an emotional discussion, in which he confronts her heterosexist assumptions and proudly reaffirms his homosexuality and his love for Richard. She apologizes and explains that she has acted as she has because she cares for him. The next morning, waiting for Richard, Martin is extremely nervous. They set off for a seaside resort. Once there, they sit in a secluded spot and talk. Richard tells of his past and then talks of the destructiveness of labelling, preferring instead to talk of caring for someone. Despite the heavy rain, they then stand together, staring out at the sea, happy at last.

The class discussion is intended to crystallize the events of the final chapter and to ask if they are what was expected. It will also be interesting to canvass predictions for Martin and Richard, now their story is over. The question, 'Who did lie inside?', is one which needs to be asked to ensure that one of the main points of the novel has been clearly understood.

After this, students return to their pressure groups, having been told that their plans of attack must be ready by the last lesson this week. They do not need to have produced anything substantive, bar the plan itself which should consist of a detailed scheme of action and a list of the materials necessary for its achievement. Execution of these schemes is to take place over the holiday, with presentations when school recommences, so letters seeking help and information need to be dispatched by the end of the week.

The book review, which is set as homework, should put the events of the novel back into context, after the fragmentary treatment they have received over the preceding six weeks. It will also allow students the opportunity to articulate their personal response both to the story itself and the issues which it raises. (Fortuitously, in the UK, such a piece fits neatly into the requirements for GCSE literature coursework.)

Week 6 Lesson 2

- Continuation of pressure group work; allowing time for students to make use of onsite facilities such as the library, resources room, computers, etc.

After their initial planning session, earlier this week, groups might well want to utilize some of the available resources within the school. They can then be directed to the appropriate place, with the injunction that they and their schemes of action must be ready for presentation by the next lesson.

Week 6 Lesson 3

- Presentation of reports from pressure groups and discussion and advice as to their implementation.
- Time for letters to be sent, etc.
- Assistance given for the completion (as a holiday assignment) of the resource pack for 13–14-year-old students. (See Week 3 Lesson 2)

The presentation of the groups' plans needs to be followed by discussion, advice and information as to how best these can be effected. It is also vital that all students share and pool their ideas and the new knowledge which they have acquired. Unless this discussion is too useful to be stopped, fifteen minutes can be set aside for groups to finish any outstanding administrative work they have.

Finally, if it is required, help can be made available for the piece of writing which students are to produce over the holidays. Their brief was to design a resource pack dealing with homosexuality, suitable for use with 13–14-year-old students as part of their sex education course. Started earlier in this unit, it is hoped that it will need updating in the light of what has since been learnt. Its purpose is to consolidate the understanding and knowledge which students now possess, by requiring that it be presented in a format both comprehensible and appropriate for 13–14-year-olds.

Further suggested activities

What follows are some additional ideas for activities which could complement or be substituted for any of those contained in the above scheme. (Similarly some of the ideas from the *Annie on my Mind* unit can be modified and used here.)

- Week 2 Lesson 1: Read the extract (Act 1, Scene 5) from Martin Sherman's play, *Bent**. Now try to continue the dialogue. Imagining that Rudy recovers, what might he say to Max? Try not to focus on any further violence – just allow Rudy and Max to talk.
- Week 2 Lesson 1: Screening of the film *November Moon**, which is the story of a lesbian couple living in France when the Nazis invade.
- Week 6: Is Linda a good friend to Martin? A chart listing the reasons for and the reasons against might help here. Read 'A bit of shrapnel' by Tom Wakefield* and then decide whether Linda is as 'good' for Martin as Aunt Bertha is for Malcolm.
- Week 6: Write the 'next chapter' of *Who Lies Inside*.
- Any time: Imagine that you write an agony column for a national newspaper. You receive a letter from a parent or friend of a young lesbian or gay man. Write both the letter which they have sent and then draft its reply. Try to be as supportive and sympathetic as possible.
- Any time: Martin has a secret which threatens to upset the course of his whole life. Write a story in which the central character is similarly affected by a secret which threatens to destabilize her/his existing way of life. (The teacher will, no doubt, want to supplement this rather bald instruction with extracts which deal with secrets and fears.)

Evaluation of scheme

This scheme has tried to include as complete a range of 'English' skills as possible, as well as a variety of different activities. Students will have been encouraged to read, write, talk and listen. The occasions for these have been reading the novel itself, a selection of poetry, extracts from other books and printed sources used for the students' independent research. As for written work, this has included informal notes and letter-writing, as well as the production of an extended informative piece, diary writing and a review. The skills of talking and listening will have been practised and extended through group work, role-play, both formal and informal discussions and during the reading of the novel itself.

The activities within the unit have been selected to exploit the range of stimuli available to the teacher of English. At the unit's completion, students will have been involved in improvisation and role-play, as well as other tasks requiring empathetic skills; pressure group simulation; writing and performing plays; reviewing and formulating both personal and critical responses across a range of different literature; the development of self-expression through poetry, imaginative, discursive and information writing; discussion and comprehension skills; as well as work which has been produced individually, in pairs and in groups.

Resource list for *Who Lies Inside* unit

Books

- *Who Lies Inside*, Timothy Ireland (London, Gay Men's Press, 1984)
- *The Naked Civil Servant*, Quentin Crisp (London, Fontana, 1977)
- *The Men with the Pink Triangles*, Heinz Heger (London, Gay Men's Press, 1986)

Short stories

- 'The cutting room', Sandy Boucher, in A. Mars-Jones (ed.) *Mae West is Dead* (London, Faber & Faber, 1983)
- 'A bit of shrapnel', Tom Wakefield, in *Drifters* (London, Gay Men's Press, 1984)

Videos and films

- *True Romance, Etc.* (Newsreel Collective); available through The Other Cinema, 79 Wardour Street, London W1
- *November Moon*, directed by Alexandra von Grote; available from the Cinema of Women, 31 Clerkenwell Close, London EC1

Other materials

- *Capital Gay*, 30 January 1987 (reproduced on p. 71)
- Selection of love poetry both lesbian and gay and straight; suggestions for appropriate lesbian and gay poetry can be found in Chapter 8

Drama

Bent by Martin Sherman (Oxford, Amber Lane Press, 1979)
Max and Rudy are gay lovers, living in Berlin during the 1930s. As a result of the Nazi persecution of lesbians and gay men, they have been arrested and are now on a train, being transported to the concentration camp, Dachau.

Act 1, Scene 5
(Sound of a train. A circle of light comes up. It is a prisoner transport train. We see one small corner. Five prisoners are in the light – two men in civilian dress, then Rudy and Max, then a man wearing a striped uniform with a pink triangle sewn on it. A guard walks through a circle of light. He carries a rifle. Silence.)

Friday
January 30th
1987

No. 277

CAPITAL GAY

THE FREE ONE

A WEEKLY NEWSPAPER PUBLISHED BY GAY MEN

Major protests after

POLICE RAID VAUXHALL

So 'good' the night

Il McI Sommerville and the Communards raised nearly £12,000 for the London Lighthouse Project, the Aids hospice, at their benefit concert on Monday night.
Helping to raise money were Erasure, The Style Council, Daryl Pandy, Carlton Edwards and Jerry and Berry who delighted the 2,000 strong crowd at the Barbican Centre, Silk Street, EC2.

MORE than 20 police raided the Royal Vauxhall Tavern in Kennington Lane, south London, on Friday night, closing the pub and arresting 11 customers and the landlord.

It is the second raid on the pub in six weeks and although there have been no charges yet, it has sent shock-waves through the gay pubs of London.

Publicans, the gay movement, local councillors, and Members of Parliament pledged their support at a meeting organised by the Gay Business Association, in the pub on Tuesday night.

Chris Smith MP (Labour, Islington North and Finsbury) told the meeting of 50 people that there were rumours of police plans to close many gay pubs and clubs in the capital, leaving "only one gay establishment in each area".

Two people told of ill-treatment when arrested by the police. Derek Smith, 27, a careers officer, suffered a strained wrist and a sprained ankle when he was hauled out of the pub at 12.45am.

Ken Comish, 31, an unemployed chef, had recently had an operation to remove the cartilage in his right knee. A

police surgeon ripped off the dressing and later sent him away with blood pouring down his leg.

Several arrested men said they were made to sign documents they weren't allowed to read. Others said they signed 'Caution Forms' agreeing they had been drunk on licensed premises. Publicans Pat and Breda McConnon fear these will be used as evidence if the police challenge their licence, as they have threatened.

Pat McConnon was also arrested for having 260 people in the pub when the fire limit is 160. There have been no charges on this or any other matter.

The pub was also raided on December 17th when police with a search warrant arrested Breda McConnon and two barstaff and took away bottles of poppers, even though they are legal. In reality, they were no longer on sale. Poppers are not illegal and the bar staff were

charges arising from this raid although the McConnons have been told to report to Kennington police on January 30th.

The Gay Business Association, the National Council for Civil Liberties and Lambeth Council are among those demanding
(Continued on Page 2)

(Continued on Page 2)

INSIDE

REGULAR FEATURES	
Postbag	2
Weekend Weather	3
Holy Matters	4
What's On	12 & 13
Arts/Entertainments	15
Television	17 & 19

ADVERTISING FEATURES	
Pubs	5 & 6
Jobs	14 & 16
Noticeboard	9
Eating Out	12
Hotels	13

CAPITAL GAY
SIX MOUNT PLEASANT
LONDON WC1X 0AP
PHONE 01 278 3764
'31 INFSJ

Keep up to date with Capital Gay every week!

(Page 2)

Vauxhall raid
(Continued from Page 1)

explanations from the police. Local MP Stuart Holland (Labour) has promised to ask Parliamentary Questions and to table a motion in the House of Commons.

One man who was in the pub on Friday has written to the police demanding explanations and estimating the latest raid will have cost more than £3,000.

Barstaff, some police officers were rubber gloves on Friday. There is speculation that this was provoked by fear and ignorance about Aids.

Breda McConnon said: "I always did support the police but I never realised what gay people must go through, until Friday night. I can honestly say I'm not very happy about them now."

Ken Comish said: "I always had a high regard for the police, but not now. You can't print what I think of them."

The GBA is writing to Metropolitan Police Commissioner Sir Kenneth Newman saying the raid was "unwarranted provocative" and damages relations between the community and the police at a time when the police have sought our help on a number of murder inquiries.

David Wilson-Carr of the Gay London Police Monitoring Group (GALOP) said: "The Met are trying to create a climate of fear. The Vauxhall was done for poppers and everybody else stopped selling them. They are trying to make us police ourselves. If we let them get away with this I don't know who's going to be next."

Chris Smith MP said: "We want to put so much pressure on them this time that they think twice about doing it again."

The Association of London Authorities and the Licensed Victuallers Association are also supporting the pub.

A committee is being organised to co-ordinate the campaign and a fighting fund is planned to help the individuals involved. The GBA is to start a pubs' section.

Anyone arrested on Friday is asked to call GALOP on 278 6215, to raise money towards formal complaints, civil action and compensation.

Rudy: Where do you think they are taking us? (Silence. The other prisoners look
away. The guard walks through the circle of light. Silence. To the prisoner
next to him:) Did you have a trial? (The prisoner doesn't answer.)

Max: Rudy! (Silence. Rudy and Max look at each other. They are both terrified.
Rudy starts to extend his hand, then withdraws it. A scream is heard off
beyond the circle. Rudy and Max look at each other, then turn away.
Silence. The guard walks through the circle of light. An SS Officer enters.
The circle slightly expands. The Officer looks at the prisoners one by one.
He stops at Rudy.)

Officer: Glasses. (Silence.) Given me your glasses. (Rudy hands the Officer his
glasses. The Officer examines them.) Horn-rimmed intelligentsia.

Rudy: What? (The Officer smiles.)

Officer: Stand up. (The guard pulls Rudy up.) Step on your glasses. (Rudy stands
petrified.) Step on them. (Rudy steps on the glasses.) Take him.

Rudy: Max! (Rudy looks at Max. The guard pulls Rudy out of the circle. Officer
smiles.)

Officer: Glasses. (He kicks the glasses away. The Officer leaves the circle of light.
The light narrows. Max stares ahead. The guard walks through the circle
of light. Silence. A scream is heard off – beyond the circle – Rudy's
scream. Max stiffens. Silence. Rudy screams again. Max moves to get up.
The man wearing the pink triangle (Horst) moves towards Max. He
touches him.)

Horst: Don't. (He removes his hand from Max and looks straight ahead. The
guard walks through the circle of light.) Don't move. You can't help him.
(Rudy screams. Silence. The guard walks through the circle of light.)

Max: This isn't happening.

Horst: It is happening.

Max: Where are they taking us?

Horst: Dachau.

Max: How do you know?

Horst: I've been through transport before. They took me to Cologne for a
propaganda film. Pink triangle in good health. Now it's back to Dachau.

Max: Pink triangle, what's that for?

Horst: Queer. If you're queer that's what you wear. If you're a Jew a yellow star.
Political – a red triangle. Criminal – green. Pink's the lowest. (He looks
straight ahead. The guard walks through the circle of light. Rudy screams.
Max starts.)

Max: This isn't happening. (Silence.) This can't be happening. (Silence.)

Horst: Listen to me. If you survive the train, you stand a chance. Here's where
they break you. You can do nothing for your friend. Nothing. If you try to
help him, they will kill you. If you even see – see what they do to him, hear –
hear what they do to him, they will kill you. If you want to stay alive, he
cannot exist. (Rudy screams.)

Max: This isn't happening. (Rudy screams.)

Horst: He hasn't a chance. He wore glasses. (Rudy screams.) If you want to stay
alive he cannot exist. (Rudy screams.) It is happening. (Horst moves away.
The light focuses in on Max's face. Rudy screams. Max stares ahead,
mumbling to himself.)

Max:	It isn't happening . . . It isn't happening. (The guard drags Rudy in. Rudy is semi-conscious. His body is bloody and mutilated. The guard holds him up. The Officer enters the circle. Max looks away. The Officer looks at Max. Max is still mumbling to himself.)
Officer:	Who is this man?
Max:	I don't know. (Max stops mumbling. He looks straight ahead.)
Officer:	Your friend? (Silence.)
Max:	No. (Rudy moans.)
Officer:	Look at him. (Max stares straight ahead.) **Look!** (Max looks at Rudy. The Officer hits Rudy. Rudy screams.) Your friend?
Max:	No. (Silence.)
Officer:	Hit him. (Max stares at the Officer.) Like this. (The Officer hits Rudy on the chest. Rudy screams.) Hit him. (Max doesn't move.) Your friend? (Max doesn't move.) Your friend?
Max:	No. (He closes his eyes. He hits Rudy.)
Officer:	Open your eyes. (Max opens his eyes.) Again. (Max hits Rudy in the chest.) Again. (Max hits Rudy again and again.) Enough. (The Officer pushes Rudy down to the ground, at Max's feet.) Your friend?
Max:	No. (The Officer smiles.)
Officer:	No. (The Officer leaves the circle of light. The guard follows him. The light focuses in – on Max's face. The train whistles. Rudy is heard, moaning, calling Max's name. The name merges with the whistle. Max takes a deep breath. Rudy calls Max's name.)
Max:	Two, three, four, five. (He takes another deep breath.) Six, seven, eight, nine, ten. (Rudy is silent. Max stares ahead.) **(Blackout.)**

Individual poems and lyrics

You are my good teachers

I am black
Our class is clever – we speak fifteen languages between us
Our form teacher is Irish
Sometimes my teacher reads African stories
Melanie called me a dirty nigger and the head-teacher sent her home

You are my good teachers

I am a girl
More than half the class are girls
I like Ms Waldron. Sometimes when we do pastoral curriculum she takes
all of us girls just with her and we can talk
I'm in the end of term play about the Suffragettes
I called Vanessa a fat slag. Don't be so sizist and sexist, she said

You are my good teachers

I think I'm gay
I know I'm the only one like that in our school
Homosexuality, lesbian, gay, queer – I looked. None of them's in the subject
index in the library

There's this teacher, Mr Dillon, every time a boy gives him trouble, this teacher, Mr Dillon, says, Sit down and shut up, you silly poof. What are you? A silly poof, sir.

I hate school

Are you my good teachers?

(Peter Bradley)

Smalltown Boy

You leave in the morning
With everything you own
In a little black case
Alone on a platform
The wind and the rain
On a sad and lonely face

Mother will never understand
Why you had to leave
For the love that you need
Will never be found at home
And the answer you seek
Will never be found at home

Pushed around and kicked around
Always a lonely boy
You were the one
That they talked about around town
As they put you down
And as hard as they would try
They'd hurt to make you cry
But you'd never cry to them
Just to your soul
No you'd never cry to them
Just to your soul
(Somerville/Steinbachek/Bronski)

28th September

Your lust
My stupidity
Was all it took
To lose my virginity.

Your longing
My craving
Left me stripped
Of the gift I was saving.

I gave everything
To satisfy your need
Not knowing that
I would be the only one to bleed.
(Jane Griffiths)

6 Case study 2: *Annie on my Mind* by Nancy Garden

Outline and plot synopsis

The novel I have chosen around which to base this second course of work is *Annie on my Mind* by Nancy Garden (first published in 1982 by the American imprint Farrar, Straus & Giroux and since 1988 available in Britain in the Virago 'Upstarts' series). In suggesting the use of this book as a class text, I am aware of some of the criticisms levelled against it, specifically in relation to its 'tweeness'. Sometimes it borders on the naive and occasionally is outright sugary. None the less, the range of teenage fiction which deals sympathetically and sensitively with lesbian issues is hardly large and, despite its faults, the book has many merits which, I hope, justify its inclusion here.

The story is told in the first person, dealing with incidents which occurred over the previous year. The narrative is interspersed with the 'present-day' reflections of the narrator, Liza Winthrop. She is 17 years old and a student at the prestigious Foster Academy, a long-established school in one of the more affluent parts of New York. Her story charts the friendship between her and Annie Kenyon, a student at a much less rarified city school. Their relationship quickly develops into one of love, which is finally expressed physically when they are asked to 'cat-sit' for two of Liza's teachers while they are on their holidays. During the time that the two young women have the house to themselves, they realize that the teachers are also lesbian lovers. A senior teacher, who lives opposite, is alerted by one of Liza's fellow students and comes to investigate. As a result of finding Liza and Annie in what she views as 'compromising' circumstances, she feels it her duty to report Liza to the Principal of Foster and a full hearing takes place. Liza lies to her parents as to the nature of her involvement with Annie. She is eventually exonerated but the two teachers are sacked. The last section of the book, which is set in the narrator's present day, describes her as she is now, at technical college and estranged from Annie, due to the pressure of the events of the preceding months. As a result of reassessing those events, Liza realizes that she still loves Annie and is now able to face the truth. She is at last able to phone her.

The book is well written and the shifts in narrative time allow students to extend their understanding of authorial perspective and narrative flow. Yet the story itself is not too complex, allowing its access across the ability range. The book is permeated with a 'niceness' which can sometimes annoy but the ending is strong, positive and neither too laboured nor too sentimental.

What follows is an annotated schema of lessons which has as its central theme *Annie on my Mind*. As with *Who Lies Inside*, the complete unit is intended to run over the period of a six-week half-term, culminating in a holiday. It is based on several assumptions, deviation from which ought not to be problematic. These include the timetabled provision of three seventy-minute lessons and one substantial piece of homework per week. A class set of the novel is available but students are not able to take them home, so all the reading has to be done in class. (Additional materials mentioned in the scheme are marked with an asterisk* and fuller details can be found at the end of this chapter, pp. 89–92).

Annie on my Mind: the scheme of work

Week 1 Lesson 1

- Hand out books. Read opening section (pp. 3–5).
- Ask students to predict what the book might be about on the basis of what they have read.
- Hand out copies of the poem, 'Lesbian'*.
- After having read the poem, students can be engaged in discussion as to what the poem is about and its different perspectives. (Alternatively it might be felt that the issues raised are more easily accessed through written responses to a number of short open-ended questions and a subsequent report back.)

The prediction exercise ought to focus them more clearly on the questions and hints which this important beginning raises, especially if students are told about it before the first section of the book is read. It is divided between first-person narrative, which is a mixture of personal reflection and the text of a never-to-be-sent letter and interludes of rare third-person narrative in which the author introduces Liza to the reader as she now is, brooding and trying not to remember. The letter, addressed to Annie, is written in such a way as to suggest a closer relationship than one of friendship and it is hoped that the ensuing predictions would bring this out.

The poem, 'Lesbian', contrasts the popular, stereotyped image of a lesbian with that which the poet believes to be the reality. It contains much startling imagery and is, in places, shocking. Yet it succinctly makes the point that lesbians are everywhere, although are not easily identifiable in the way which the public conception of them as political, butch, men-haters might lead one to believe. As was indicated, it might be felt that students would engage better with the material if their responses were sought to a number of structured, textual questions rather than in open, whole-class discussion. Given the taboo nature of the subject matter and the possible embarrassment of some students and the antipathy of others, it might be more constructive, so early in the issue's airing, to follow this former course.

Week 1 Lesson 2

- Read Chapters 1 and 2 (pp. 7–25).
- Ask students to fill in a character chart for each of the major characters introduced so far.

The opening chapter of the novel describes Liza's first meeting with Annie in the Metropolitan Museum of Art. She overhears a girl singing and they start talking, their conversation taking the form of 'Medieval' play-acting, as if to cover some embarrassment which is inexplicable to Liza, but is none the less enjoyable. They use the museum's exhibits as a backcloth against which to play out their fantasies, drawing a certain amount of (male) public attention to themselves. Throughout, Liza is much more inhibited and aware of other people's reactions than Annie, yet when they leave to go their separate ways, some kind of connection appears to have been established between them. They swap phone numbers and Liza is conscious of feeling that 'something important had happened'.

Chapter 2 is set the following day at Liza's school. Through what she sees as luck, she was recently elected president of the school's student council. On her way to a class, she discovers an unauthorized and fairly barbaric ear-piercing clinic, run by a fellow student, Sally. She checks to make sure that basic sanitary standards are being maintained and makes her way to her next class. That afternoon, she is summoned to see the Principal, Mrs Poindexter, and the indication is that it concerns the large number of bloody paper tissues, being held to earlobes, with which the school now abounds!

The decision to ask students to complete a character chart for each of the characters is made for three reasons. The first is that the book takes some while before getting into the 'guts' of the story. Second, as a result, the first three chapters concentrate on building up portraits of the characters who are to feature in the main action. It is therefore important for students to have a clear understanding of these characters, so that the motives for their subsequent conduct are easier to explain. Third, it is felt that after the 'overtness' of the initial raising of the concept of lesbianism in the first lesson, the aims of the course would be best served by backgrounding the issue and allowing the book to reintroduce it during the course of its unfolding narrative, so as neither to distort its progress nor pre-empt its action. To that end, the remaining activities for the week have no specific, overt lesbian or gay 'content'.

Week 1 Lesson 3

- Read Chapters 3 and 4 (pp. 26–48).
- Class discussion on the issue of student politics and teacher autonomy.

- Set homework, which is for students to find a poem which is in some way relevant or important to them. Their choice should be 'justified' in a piece of writing explaining why they chose it and how it affects them.

Chapter 3 deals with Liza's interview with Mrs Poindexter. The latter is portrayed as extremely old-fashioned and autocratic. She plays on the fact that Foster Academy is under the threat of closure due to financial difficulties and suggests that if the news that students were mutilating one another were to become public knowledge, the fund-raising campaign, orchestrated by the father of one of the 'victims', would undoubtedly suffer. She announces that a disciplinary hearing, to examine the conduct of both Sally and Liza herself, will take place the following week. When she arrives home, Liza is pleased to find a message that Annie phoned; 'it was the best thing that had happened all day'.

Chapter 4 begins with an English lesson in which the teacher is discussing William Henley's poem, 'Invictus'. Later, the action moves to the hearing. The undemocratic nature of Mrs Poindexter is further revealed as the hearing progresses. Her eventual decision is that both Liza and Sally are to be suspended for a week and, due to the former's position as president of the student council, a vote of confidence will be held.

In suggesting a further reading from the book, I am aware that this will mean that four chapters will have been covered within the space of one week. However, these are short chapters. Also, as was pointed out above, the book is relatively slow to start and, given what might well be a strong student antipathy to its subject matter, it is important to move towards the main story as quickly as possible. For these reasons, the ensuing discussion, based on student politics and teacher power, ought to provide the students with the opportunity to voice their own views on a subject which is not greatly contentious.

The homework, that students find and explain the choice of a poem which is in some way relevant or important to them, is dependent not only upon the availability of a wide selection of poetry anthologies, mirroring both heterosexual and lesbian and gay life-styles, as well as those dealing with the experiences of women and Black people, but also upon students possessing a fair degree of autonomy in the field of reading and understanding poetry on their own.

Week 2 Lesson 1

- Read Chapter 5 and the following 'present-day' section (pp. 49–67).
- Write a description of how an outsider might see your school.

Chapter 5 tells of the reaction of Liza's parents to her suspension, which they see as fair. She spends the next day with Annie, who cannot believe that Liza has been suspended for something she considers to be so trivial, especially in comparison to her own school experience. Once again, they revert to play-acting. The next day, Liza goes out for a walk and bumps into Annie. She invites her back for supper and shows her around her room. Liza's father, herself and her brother offer to take Annie home. Once they arrive in her neighbourhood, she is clearly embarrassed by its meanness in comparison to the Winthrop's. The remaining 'present-day' section contains a further description of Liza, as she is now, trying hard to forget, but still being able only to remember.

Later on in the book, Liza visits Annie's school and is amazed at how it differs from her own. It might therefore be useful, at this point, for students to evaluate how an outsider, whether human or alien, might view the school world they know so well and whose idiosyncrasies they accept almost without question.

Week 2 Lesson 2

● Screen the video *First Feelings**.
● Class discussion on issues raised, focusing particularly on family reaction.

The *First Feelings* video, which was produced by the 'Relationships and Sexuality' project set up by ILEA, is a twenty-minute documentary which talks to young lesbians and gay men and their families about the impact upon each of them when they first discovered or were told about the young person's homosexuality. It is a very touching film which contains much that is very positive, particularly from the relatives of the young people. The video has worked very well in a number of schools and is almost guaranteed to raise a number of important issues. It is hoped that students will want to cover a lot of ground and, while ensuring that this is possible, the teacher ought to attempt, first, to limit the instances of unhelpful homophobic abuse, and second, to highlight the role their family has to play in a person's decision as to whether or not to come out. There is work in Week 3 which will pick up on this latter area.

Week 2 Lesson 3

● Read Chapter 6 and the following 'present-day' section (pp. 69–95).
● Distribute 'Sexuality' worksheet* and ask students to fill it in. They are then to work in groups and aim to achieve a consensus for each statement. There should then be space for each group to report back their decisions.
● For homework, students ought to write an imaginary letter to an agony column, in which the writer is having difficulties coming to terms with her/his sexuality.

Chapter 6, which is quite short, describes Liza's visit to Annie's school, a place worlds apart from Foster Academy. Later that day, as arranged, she visits her apartment, bringing her an African Violet. There she meets Annie's grandmother who thanks her for making her Annie happy. They sit and talk. Annie is moved by the gift and tells Liza about her life before she came to New York. The next day, which is Thanksgiving, finds the Winthrops just finishing their meal, when at the door are Annie and her father, asking if the Winthrops would like to join their family for a drive. Only Liza chooses to go. Finally, after a brief (and fairly pappy) reflection about how one person can feel so close to another, 'that you can't understand why you and the other person have separate bodies, separate skins' (!), the book tells of the day when Liza first felt this about Annie. They sit on a pier and kiss. They then pull away, leaving Liza confused but convinced of her feelings for Annie. The present-day section has Liza crumpling up a half-written letter to Annie and thinking back.

The 'Sexuality' worksheet, which should initially be done individually, requires students to indicate whether they agree or disagree with several statements relating to lesbians and gay men. It was designed for a Personal and Health Education lesson for 13–14-year-olds and works very well. There is deliberately no space for students *not* to express an opinion, as it is important that they confront each of these statements, without there being a let-out clause. Further, a 'Don't know' option would make the subsequent consensus exercise difficult. Its purpose is to get students to discuss the issues raised without being inhibited by what some of them might see as the intrusive presence of a teacher. The report-back should include skilful, non-confrontational questioning of some of the decisions reached. While a number of the statements have no definitive answers, some do have factual (dis)proofs and these ought to be made clear.

For homework, students are to write an imaginary letter to an agony column, in which the writer is having difficulties coming to terms with her/his sexuality. Again the fictional nature of the piece needs to be emphasized. When these are collected in the following week, students will be given a letter, which is not their own, and asked to produce a helpful, honest reply.

Week 3 Lesson 1

- Read Chapter 8 (pp. 97–106).
- Discussion of variety of terms used to discuss sexual orientation.
- Ask students, in groups to 'brainstorm' around the question 'What does it mean to be lesbian or gay?'
- As a whole class, try to prioritize the top five statements.
- Collect in the homework set in Week 2 Lesson 3.

Chapter 8 is set in the week following Thanksgiving. Back at school, the vote of confidence takes place and Liza retains her position as president of the student council. She phones Annie and, at the latter's request, goes round. Once there, Annie gives Liza a letter and leaves her to read it. In it, she acknowledges that she is, in her words, 'gay' and that she loves her but neither wants to influence her nor see her remain involved in something with which she cannot cope. On Annie's return, Liza says that were it not the first letter which Annie had ever written to her, she would rip it up. The chapter ends with them embracing, happy yet scared.

In her letter, Annie uses the word 'gay' and suggests that it is something to which Liza has not yet given much thought. This seems an ideal opportunity to raise the variety of terms used to describe sexuality. The subsequent brainstorming activity is then intended to focus students on the differences which exist (or which they believe exist) for lesbian and gay young people compared to their heterosexual peers. When it comes to the class prioritization of the statements chosen, it is hoped that the discussion of those to be included will lead to a deeper understanding of the situation in which such young people find themselves.

The homework, set at the end of the previous week, needs to be collected and marked before the next lesson where it is to be handed back out.

Week 3 Lesson 2

● Hand out marked 'agony' letters, ensuring that no one receives her/his own. Students are to write a response, in role as an agony columnist, suggesting useful, practical advice.
● Encourage students to read out their letters and responses.

The purpose of this lesson is, by putting students in role, to allow them to express the sorts of opinions whose articulation, in a less disguised forum, might be hindered due to peer pressure. This is not fool-proof; the original writers will still be recognizable, but may well feel better protected. While they are writing, the teacher ought to be aware of those letters and their replies which it would be of value to share later.

Again, as the views have been partially distanced from their writers, when it comes to letters being read out, students, particularly the original letter writers themselves, will benefit from having the opportunity to suggest alternative advice or information.

Week 3 Lesson 3

● Read Chapter 9 (pp. 107–23).
● Students are to write a piece of dialogue between a teenager and her/his closest adult relative, in which the young person 'comes out'. They should be encouraged to take on the role of a teenager of the opposite sex to their own.

Chapter 9 describes the growth of Liza and Annie's relationship during that winter. At Christmas they find that each has bought the other a similar ring. Throughout this time, they never talk of what it is that they are, focusing instead on their day-to-day lives. It is this inability to talk about their sexuality which leads to the build up of tension between them. Rows follow one another and result in a much more serious argument which takes some while to settle. Eventually they sit down and discuss the cause of their frustration and their mutual fear of sexual contact. They decide they both need more time and chances to talk to allay these fears.

It would seem that the cause of the problem which faces Liza and Annie is their inability to give a name to their love or, indeed, to themselves. The dialogue work is intended to make students realize the difficulty inherent in finding a solution to this problem and also to allow them to articulate their own feelings and responses to such a situation. There are two reasons that students are to take on a character with a different gender from their own. The first is an attempt to lessen any causes for embarrassment or the influence of peer group pressure, by depersonalizing the work from students' own experience. The second is to try to remove the possibility of there being any 'threat' for those students who still fear homosexuality. This would clearly stop them from being able to empathize with an individual whom they resent. It is important that these students are given an opportunity to take part as it is they who, after all, would most obviously benefit from such an exercise. By adopting the persona of a completely different individual, it is hoped that this will provide them with less cause to feel threatened.

Week 4 Lesson 1

- Read Chapter 10 (pp. 124–38).
- Whole class discussion regarding the school's role in shielding its students, broadening out into an examination of state and private education.

Chapter 10 concerns an emergency council meeting which Mrs Poindexter calls in order to discuss ways in which the student body can help the fund-raising campaign. It is held at the home of two of the staff, Ms Widmer and Ms Stevenson. Before the meeting starts, the former asks Liza if she would look after their cats while she and Ms Stevenson are away on holiday. Once it gets underway, the meeting is as undemocratic and unconstitutional as usual, due to Mrs Poindexter's increasing despotism. The members get bogged down, discussing the merits and detriments of a Foster education compared to one offered at a (public) state school. Eventually it is decided to hold a large public rally the following week. The meeting ends with Mrs Poindexter and her side-kick, Ms Baxter, giving a highly charged rendition of one of the school songs!

The next activity is based around the issue of private versus state education. This is a subject which is often covered in schools and is included here, not only to provide an alternative topic for students to work with to avoid overload, but also to allow them the opportunity, in a less contentious area, to practise the difficult skill of writing discursively. As a starting-point, it might be worth looking at how far schools should shield their students from the outside world. This can then be widened to include the differences which have been perceived between the two education philosophies from the book. Finally, students ought then to be able to give their own views about the pros and cons of each system as they relate to them.

Week 4 Lesson 2

- Continue with examination of the 'education debate'.
- Set up discursive essay to be completed for homework.

This lesson gives the teacher the chance to feed in a range of resources and stimuli to ensure that students have sufficient information upon which to base a discursive essay. Its title and additional stimuli can be drawn from a fusion of the resources available and the direction which the discussions take. The essay is to be completed for homework.

Week 4 Lesson 3

- Read Chapters 11 and 12 (pp. 139–51).
- Ask students to produce an encyclopaedia entry for the word 'homosexuality'.

Chapter 11 finds both Liza and Annie accepted at their chosen colleges. They go for a walk and discuss their sexual frustration, caused by their having no place where they are able to be alone. Later that night, when she is back at home, Liza looks up 'homosexuality' in her father's encyclopaedia and is furious that it makes no mention of love. The next day, Annie gives her a copy of *Patience and Sarah* (see appendix, p. 121) to read and their quest of lesbian and gay literature is born.

Chapter 12 describes the days Liza and Annie spent at the teachers' house while cat-sitting. Without becoming graphic, Garden builds up the young women's growing sense of physical intimacy and knowledge of one another, as they become more comfortable. It is hoped that over the last four weeks students will have gained enough knowledge to be able to write an encyclopaedia definition for homosexuality which might not mortify Liza. Perhaps students might benefit from seeing a particularly unsympathetic entry before they begin their own. (In the absence of locating anything more outrageous, the resource list which follows this unit contains an extract from the Medical Matters section of the *Pears Cyclopaedia* for 1974–5.)

Week 5 Lesson 1

- Read Chapter 13, the following 'present-day' section and Chapter 14 (pp. 152–72).
- Provoke discussion of the place of lesbian and gay teachers, bringing in Section 28 and its background.
- For homework, in play form, students are to produce the conversation which is to take place between Ms Widmer, Ms Stevenson, Liza and Annie.

Although much happens, the three recommended extracts from the book are short and to split them up would have a detrimental effect upon the tension and excitement which Garden creates. In Chapter 13 Liza and Annie, while searching for the cat, come across the teachers' bedrooms. They discover that there is only one which has a bed in it and that, coupled with an examination of that room's bookshelves, makes them realize that Ms Widmer and Ms Stevenson are lovers. They talk about how they don't want to keep their lives secret but are hindered by the presence of the bed. They resist it, but are unable to continue their conversation. Two days later, which is their last 'in charge' of the house, to cover the tension that has grown up, they revert to their old role-playing. This leads to a mock sword fight and a chase, which leaves them breathless, upstairs, lying on the bed. They then begin to make love and, far below, hear the front door rattle.

The 'present-day' section consists of another of Liza's half-started-never-to be-sent letters to Annie. In it, she asserts poignantly that 'love is good as long as it's honest and unselfish and hurts no one'. It is the final clause against which Liza is still stumbling and which has stopped her contacting Annie since the previous June.

Chapter 14 takes us back to the front door rattling. Someone calls for the door to be opened or the police will be called. When Liza opens it, she finds Ms Baxter and her fellow student, Sally. The newcomers head for the stairs and see Annie, naked but for her jacket. Ms Baxter begins wailing and denouncing, with fundamentalist fervour, the 'Sodom and Gomorrah' which she and Sally have uncovered. At this point, Ms Widmer and Ms Stevenson return and, after listening to a now almost hysterical and insulting Ms Baxter, they ask her to leave and take Sally with her. This she does but with the parting shot that she considers it her duty to report all *four* of them to Mrs Poindexter. Following their departure, Liza and Annie are told by Ms Widmer and Ms Stevenson to get dressed and to return to the kitchen to discuss what has happened.

The following discussion is intended to tackle the prejudice which loudly proclaims that lesbians and gay men are not fit to be teachers. (A number of short, first-hand accounts from teachers, at varying stages of 'out'-ness, have been written and a list of where these can be located is in the resource list, following this unit. Teachers might also want to adapt extracts from the sections of Chapter 7 of this book which deal specifically with the role of lesbian and gay teachers.) Once again, recent statistics relating to child sex abuse will need to be provided to destroy the pernicious belief that all gay men are paedophiles and that lesbians desire only to 'convert' heterosexual girls. It might also be of use to widen the discussion out to include Section 28 and its intention to prohibit exactly the sort of lessons which students have been experiencing during the course of the previous five weeks.

As homework, students are to predict the conversation which is to take place, in the following chapter, between Ms Widmer, Ms Stevenson, Liza and Annie. It ought to take the form of a play and students ought to try to bring the personality of each character through what each says.

Week 5 Lesson 2

- Read 'The two spinster ladies'*.
- Through a series of structured questions, students should look at what the

story has to say about female sexuality and the assumptions which are often made about it.

The short story, 'The two spinster ladies', describes the shock given to one of a coterie of 'coffee-morning ladies', Mrs Jenkins, when she pays a visit on two of the others, who live together. She finds them standing 'rather too close to one another' and so naked that 'neither of them . . . even had her earrings on'. She immediately suspects witchcraft and informs the other ladies. At their next coffee morning, the two 'witches' are asked to explain their conduct. They say that they were performing their regular exercises, as recommended by Swiss doctors. This, they claim, is the secret of their youthfulness. Their explanation is completely accepted and it is Mrs Jenkins who is made to feel embarrassed by her stupid assumption.

Through the use of humour, the story makes the point that women are rarely allowed to have a sexuality, and never if it is not in relation to men. The subsequent questions ought to provoke students to considering why this might be, why women are expected to be more reserved in discussing sex and why sex is often perceived as a male action. Students could also be asked why the following words have no direct male or female equivalent and what each connotes about the person it seeks to describe.

spinster	mistress	slag	tart
nymphomaniac	Casanova	slut	stud

Week 5 Lesson 3

- Read Chapter 15 (pp. 173–94).
- After a short discussion, which should focus on the likely participants in the hearing, students should go off in groups of between ten or twelve and work on producing a realistic 'trial' scene, which is to be videoed the following week.

In Chapter 15 Liza and Annie are now dressed and come back down to the kitchen to talk to Ms Widmer and Ms Stevenson. Each pair is either too embarrassed or too angry for there to be any real discussion, so they arrange to meet the next day. On this occasion, they are more relaxed. They realize that Liza's parents will have to know. On their way home, Liza and Annie argue because of the latter's refusal to tell her parents as well. This disagreement is soon made up. The next day Liza is summoned to Mrs Poindexter. The latter claims that Liza's conduct is pure ingratitude and feels that she has no choice but to suspend her, pending an expulsion hearing. She also promises to telephone her parents as soon as their interview is over. The chapter is then interrupted by the present-day Liza reflecting on what fairness and immorality really are.

Back to the past and, on clearing her locker, Liza discovers it contains a homophobic note. When she gets home, she lies to her mother, who has been crying, and is prompted, by her mother's soothing use of the 'it's only a phase' argument, to say that what transpired between her and Annie was no more than 'normal' teenage sexual experimentation. Her father offers his support whatever, but the tolerance which he had displayed in the past towards homosexuality seems to have waned. Next day, when she sees Sally, she is met with condemnation and more religious fervour and the news that Ms Widmer and Ms Stevenson have also been suspended.

Despite the fact that theirs is a separate hearing, in order to allow students the chance to discuss the appropriate fate of Ms Widmer and Ms Stevenson, the role-play ought to place them alongside Liza as defendants. The groups need to be large, so as to take in all the possible witnesses and participants. These would need to include Ms Widmer, Ms Stevenson, Liza herself, Ms Baxter, Sally, Mrs Poindexter, defence and prosecution counsel and a chair of trustees who will preside. Other witnesses can be used and 'spare' students can take on the role of jurors. More preparation time will be available in Week 6 and, as a result of being told that their work will be videoed when it is presented, students ought to be well motivated and produce thoughtful and empathetic responses.

Week 6 Lesson 1

- Allow more time to rehearse 'hearing' plays.
- Show and video these.

If students have organized themselves well, it ought to be possible to provide some space for last-minute rehearsal and still have sufficient time for each group to show their work. If this is not the case (as it often isn't!), then time can be set aside later in the week for the filming, albeit at the expense of subsequent activities.

Week 6 Lesson 2

- Read Chapter 16 (pp. 195–211).
- Produce, in writing, the verdict of the hearing. This can be either by Mr Turner or Mrs Poindexter.

Chapter 16 deals almost exclusively with Liza's hearing. It is prefaced by her discovery that her younger brother Chad, has been questioned by Mrs Poindexter about her past liaisons, both male and female. Just before the hearing, Liza promises Annie that it will make no difference to their relationship and, as she says it, she knows that she is lying to her as well.

Once the hearing gets underway, Liza is unsure what is actually on trial. Ms Baxter gives her evidence and is unable not to make swingeing accusations concerning Ms Widmer and Ms Stevenson, despite the fact that they are not themselves on trial at this point. The chair of trustees, Mr Foster, corrects this and a number of the interruptions which Mrs Poindexter feels forced to make. When asked if she actually saw Liza and Annie touch each other in a sexual way,

Ms Baxter is forced to reply in the negative. Liza is then questioned but is unable to explain why she and Annie were only partially clothed. Her mother interrupts and is then shouted down by Mrs Poindexter. Finally, one of the trustees exclaims that the whole thing is getting out of hand. She argues that what Liza does in her own spare time is the sole concern of her and her parents. She goes on to say that the only worrying aspect of the hearing is Mrs Poindexter's pursuance of the matter in the form of a near-vendetta. She reminds her colleagues that this is not the first time that the Principal has acted in this way and that the issue is whether Ms Widmer and Ms Stevenson exerted any influence on Liza. So, after asking Liza if she has anything more she wants to say, Mr Turner brings the hearing to a close.

The purpose of asking students to produce the verdict of the hearing is to force them to evaluate the evidence *and* decide what actually is on trial. The choice, of whether to write as Mr Foster or Mrs Poindexter, is provided so that, whatever the verdict, it can be given an appropriate mouthpiece.

Week 6 Lesson 3

• Read Chapter 17 to the end of the book (pp. 212–34).
• Discuss the ending, both in terms of its strengths and weaknesses.
• Set up final assignment to be done over the holidays.

Chapter 17 documents the arrival of Liza's letter of exoneration and her subsequent return to school. Apart from one of her fellow students asking the age-old question, 'What do two girls do in bed?', most people are friendly. She finds out from Sally that Mrs Poindexter is to be replaced in the next academic year but that Ms Widmer and Ms Stevenson have been dismissed. Sally also says that she was present at the latter's hearing, where she testified to Liza's idolization of them and their consequent influence over her. . . . This is then followed by another section of Liza's 'present-day' reflection, dealing with how she might have saved the teachers if she had been at their hearing. She ends, driving herself on to climb that last mountain.

Chapter 18 describes Liza and Annie visiting Ms Widmer and Ms Stevenson for the last time. They are full of guilt and regret for what they have done to the two women's careers. Ms Widmer and Ms Stevenson tell them of how *they* were told not to see each other when they were Liza and Annie's age. They urge them to believe that the worst thing which can happen is for them to be separated. The final two pages take place in Liza's present day and show her finally realizing that 'the truth makes one free'. She is now able to phone Annie and tell her that she loves her.

Students will obviously want to express immediate opinions once the book has been finished and space should be made here for them to do so. Discussion ought to include its structure and the ending. (It might also be worth asking students how they think that one of their colleagues might fare on her/his return after having been in a similar position to Liza.) The final assignment, to be completed over the forthcoming holidays, is a choice between a literature-based book review, which none the less looks at the appropriateness of the inclusion of lesbian issues in a book for young adults, and an imaginative piece which portrays the lives which Ms Widmer and Ms Stevenson led before coming to Foster or those which they will now lead.

Further suggested activities

What follows are some additional ideas for activities which could complement or be substituted for any of those contained in the above scheme. Appropriate ideas from the *Who Lies Inside* scheme can also be used.

• Week 1 Lesson 2: Given that students had to justify and explain their choice of poem, if it appears to be appropriate and students give their permission, it might be entertaining and of some use to provide each with another's choices and see if they can work out whose it is.
• Week 5 Lesson 1: Read 'Nothing like' by Rodney Mills* and then write the memo that the teacher, Geoff Grant, might put in Barry Walsh's file. Now write Geoff's diary, covering the interview with Barry.
• Any time: Screening of the film *November Moon**, which is the poignant story of a lesbian couple living in France when the Nazis invade.
• Any time: Read *Lesbian Mothers on Trial: A Report on Lesbian Mothers and Child Custody**. Produce a newspaper feature, using a maximum of 500 words, on the problems faced by lesbian mothers and their children.
• Any time: As with the *Who Lies Inside* unit, students can be encouraged to put together a resource booklet on homosexuality for use with a lower school class.
• Any time: Liza very nearly destroys the best thing that has ever happened to her, by being more concerned about other people's views than she is about her own happiness. Write a story in which you or the central character is torn between doing the 'right thing' and following what it is which s/he knows is what would make her/him happy.

Evaluation of scheme

As with the *Who Lies Inside* unit, this scheme has tried to include as wide a range of English skills as possible, as well as a number of different activities. Students will have been encouraged to read, write, talk and listen. The occasions for these have been reading the novel itself, pieces of information writing, a short story and some poetry. As for written work, this has ranged from informal notes, to a piece suitable for inclusion in an encyclopaedia, as well as the production of an extended discursive essay, letter writing and a review. The skills of talking and listening will have been utilized and, I hope, extended through the group work, both formal and informal discussions, role-play and during the reading of the novel itself.

The activities within the unit have been selected both to demonstrate and to exploit the range of stimuli available to the teacher of English. At the unit's completion, students will have been involved in improvisation and role-play, in addition to other tasks requiring empathetic skills; the writing and performance of plays; reviewing and formulating both personal and critical responses across a variety of literature; the development of self-expression across a range of media; imaginative, discursive and information writing; discussion and comprehension skills; as well as work which has been produced individually, in pairs and in groups.

Resource list for *Annie on my Mind* unit

Books

- *Annie on my Mind*, Nancy Garden (London, Virago Upstarts, 1988)
- *Lesbian Mothers on Trial: A Report on Lesbian Mothers and Child Custody* (London, Rights of Women, 1986)

Short stories

- 'The two spinster ladies', Kate Hall, in J. Bradshaw and M. Hemming (eds) *Girls Next Door: Lesbian Feminist Stories* (London, The Women's Press, 1985).
- 'Nothing like', Rodney Mills, in D. Rees and P. Robins (eds) *Oranges and Lemons: Stories by Gay Men* (London, Third House, 1987).

Autobiographical accounts of teachers, relating to coming out at school

- 'A teacher or a gay man vs. a gay man as a teacher', John, in *Outlaws in the Classroom: Lesbians and Gays in the School System* (Lesbian and Gay Working Party of the City of Leicester Teachers' Association (NUT), 1987)
- 'I don't want to whisper anymore', Lena, ibid.
- 'One foot out of the closet', Terry, ibid.
- 'Inn and out', Peter Bradley, in *School's Out* (London, Gay Teachers' Group, 1987)
- 'Coming out experiences', Geoff Hardy and others, ibid.

Videos and films

- *First Feelings*, ILEA; available from CLR, 275 Kennington Lane, London SE11 5QZ
- *November Moon*, directed by Alexandra von Grote; available from the Cinema of Women, 31 Clerkenwell Close, London EC1

Other materials

• Large selection of poetry anthologies, mirroring both heterosexual and lesbian and gay experiences
• Worksheets

'Sexuality' worksheet
Look carefully at the following statements and then tick those ones you agree with and put a cross next to those with which you disagree.

                                                    Agree   *Disagree*

1 One in ten of the population is lesbian or gay
2 Lesbians and gays should be locked up
3 Lesbians and gays should have the same rights
  as everyone else
4 Gay men molest children
5 I find homosexuality disgusting
6 People are only prejudiced against lesbians
  and gay men because they don't know enough
  about them
7 Lesbians hate men
8 Lesbians and gay men are born, not made
9 Lesbians only 'do it' because they can't find a
  man
10 Lesbians and gay men could be straight if they
   tried
11 Lesbians hate children

Now, in your groups, try to work out a set of consensus responses so that each member of your group agrees with the overall decision.

• Encyclopaedia definition

Encyclopaedia definition of 'homosexuality'
Extract from the Medical Matters section of the *Pears Cyclopaedia* for 1974–5, for possible use in Week 4 Lesson 3

> **Homosexuality** is, as presumably most people now know, an attraction between individuals of the same sex. Most people pass through a brief homosexual stage. Ordinarily, this comes just before puberty when schoolgirls get 'crushes' on older girls or teachers and schoolboys have similar feelings towards their heroes. The disposition, however, may be retained into adult life. Nowadays people take a much more tolerant view of homosexuality, accepting that what adults do (with consent) is their own business and that a male homosexual who seduces a boy under age should be treated in no way differently from the man who seduces an under-age girl. Male homosexual practices are no longer an offence if committed in private between consenting adults. Female homosexual practices have never been an offence.

The following questions could well be raised in relation to this definition.

1 What kind of 'attraction' does the writer mean?
2 What evidence does s/he have to support the statement that 'Most people pass through a brief homosexual stage'?
3 What kind of tolerance does the writer mean?
4 Why does s/he mention paedophilia when it is a well-known fact that 93 per cent of all sexual abuse of children is perpetrated by a *heterosexual* male member of the victim's family (City of Leicester Teachers' Association 1988)?
5 What does the verb 'committed' mean when talking about gay male sex? Do heterosexuals commit intercourse?
6 Why has lesbian sex never been included within the criminal law?

Individual poems

Lesbian

YOUR IMAGE:
I am a lesbian
I open cans with my teeth.
I have a domineering mother,
except when I have a domineering father,
sister, brother, school-friend, neighbour, gay man who came to read the gas meter
when I was six.
I creep out
at the dead of night
to steal men's underpants
which I wear – under my tweed skirt.
I live at Greenham
except when I live next door to you.
I go to drop-in-centres
for left-wing-commie-cigar-smoking-butch-bulldykes-against-the-bomb
paid for by the GLC.
I have fourteen fingers
we grow extra ones
you know.
I leap out from under 'man'hole covers
to grab 'straight' women
And I'm secretly plotting with Russia
to 'dis-arm' Ronald Reagan.

HOW IT IS:
You've never quite got it right
about me
So let me tell you about myself.
I am complicated but
surprisingly average.

I do everything
and as for jobs:
I have a good job, a bad job, no job
I'm fired from jobs, I create jobs
I've worked just about any kind of job you can think of
except Prime Minister
unfortunately.

I am a thousand colours
and come from a thousand places
I come in a thousand places
and out in a thousand places.

I am behind you in the bus queue,
the cinema, the supermarket.
I live everywhere
except Buckingham Palace
as far as I know.

I am older than spoken word
traces of my bones lie in the stones
beneath your feet.
I am made of rock
harder than diamond
It cuts through your conventions
and your sticky, sticky lies.

I am more women than you would believe
and more woman than you would understand.

What am I?

Caroline Claxton

7 Splendid isolation or in concert?

Throughout the previous four chapters, the major, almost exclusive, thrust of this book's arguments has been towards the acceptance of the English classroom as an ideal site for ideological and social change. It has been argued that, as can be seen from anti-racist and anti-sexist initiatives, English is by far the most amenable and appropriate area in which to begin to tackle issues of prejudice. Research, the national curriculum, individual works of literature, all have been invoked in order to attempt to cajole even the most reluctant English department into accepting what, it has been suggested, is the responsibility of all. This chapter moves on to discuss the wider repercussions of a policy of anti-heterosexist education, in respect of both the teachers who undertake it and in the context of the whole school itself. Its intention is to examine the viability of an individual department or, less satisfactorily, an individual teacher attempting to introduce changes in this area, while acting in isolation. Following on from this, the chapter then looks at the possibility of whole school initiatives, focusing particularly on the use of policy documents and the respective role of parents, school governors and the pastoral curriculum. Finally, it will attempt to grapple with the thorny issue of the rights and duties of lesbian and gay teachers.

Splendid isolation? The brave individual

Nothing would be more satisfying to the author of this book than to know that in response to its arguments a number of its readers were now committed to re-evaluating their current practices and fully intended to tackle homophobia head on. (The purpose of the book has been to achieve just that.) However, within a very short space of time, teachers who do choose to follow such a course of action will no doubt realize the enormity of their task. Almost immediately, they will stumble across one of the three major pitfalls waiting to trip up the concerned teacher. The first is the reactions of students. The second is the school hierarchy's response to these and their own reactions, while the final problem is the difficulty of resourcing.

'Miss is a lesbian'

> Being assertive in the classroom, refusing to be flirted with, challenging any sexist or
> heterosexist comments, I am still described as 'being like a man'. As a lesbian teacher
> I am also taunted by the images of so-called 'lesbian behaviour' which the boys (and
> the staff?) have culled from pornographic videos and magazines.
>
> (Anonymous 1989: 156)

Because of its allegedly 'sensitive' nature, individual teachers who begin work in
this area run the risk of placing themselves on the 'front line', when raising the
issue of lesbian and gay sexuality. It will be seen as that particular teacher's
hobby-horse and students will begin to question why this is. A white, male
teacher, committed to both anti-racist and anti-sexist teaching strategies, is
hardly likely to be called either a nigger or a slag. However, any teacher dealing
sympathetically with homosexuality is immediately a dyke or a pansy. (What
assumptions has the reader made about the sexuality of the author? Why *should*
that necessarily be the case?)

Recently, a colleague was amazed to hear a senior lecturer in Psychology draw
a distinction between homophobia and other manifestations of prejudice, on the
basis of which she felt confidence in expressing the view that lesbians and gay men
are less oppressed than other groups in society. This was justified by virtue of the
fact that lesbians and gay men have the positive choice to hide those facets of
themselves which are considered to be socially unacceptable and give rise to their
oppression. This, she said, was a choice unavailable to women and Black people.
For that reason, the prejudice they encounter is of a different nature from either
racism or sexism, in that it contains an element of complicity. Apart from its
obvious logical inconsistencies in relation to the experiences of *all* lesbians and of
Black and Asian gay men, the argument is an extremely crude and patronising
attempt to peddle self-regulation. What it says is, 'allow us to perceive that there
is no difference between us and we will indeed perceive that there is no
difference'. As was mentioned earlier, to prioritize manifestations of discrimination, to remove them from the political equation which ensures that prejudice
always equals power, is to isolate actions which are specifically designed to form
part of a cohesive whole.

However, hidden beneath this spurious argument, is a germ of the reality of the
lives of lesbians and gay men. This can broadly be expressed as an overwhelming
presumption of heterosexuality until proven otherwise (or guilty). The lesbian or
gay man, with the exception of those whose natural demeanour conforms to
crude, homophobic stereotypes, will be able to pass for straight if s/he so chooses.
What constitutes 'proof' of homosexuality will depend upon those stereotypes
currently in circulation within society at large. Whether these are postural, such
as a nonconformity to accepted gender roles, or involve assuming particular
articles of clothing, their adoption will alert others that that person's sexuality is
up for question.

But perhaps the most obvious evidence of homosexuality, prized by a heterosexist society, is to show tolerance towards it. Unlike every other expression of prejudice, with the possible exception of that held in relation to political groups who have not eschewed violence, the levels of homophobia are so high in Britain that anything short of total contempt for or outright dismissal of the issue is likely to reward its supporter with a strong implication of compliance.

For a teacher, irrespective of her/his own sexual orientation, to begin the process of defusing homophobia in the classroom will be tantamount to an open declaration of, at the very least, sexual ambiguity. Many will have already constructed pre-existing indices of heterosexuality which may counter-balance this assumption, but for others it will prompt an extremely difficult question which has no obvious answer. 'Are you a lesbian, Miss?' Now, if the answer is yes, then is it right, both for the teacher herself and her students, to answer honestly? (This dilemma is examined in more detail below.) If the answer is 'no', what connotation does such a reply have? Will it just reinforce the prejudices of some students? What effect will it have on lesbian and gay students within the class? What does a direct 'no' say about that teacher's own attitudes? What else is there she could say?

Therefore the likely result of even an attempt to deal sympathetically with aspects of sexuality will be some re-evaluation of students' relationship with their teacher, which, in some ways, is no bad thing. Sensitively handled, this should pose few real problems. The real areas of difficulty relate to the issue of whether a teacher ought to come out if asked and the problems of dealing with homophobic abuse once sexuality has been introduced into the realm of classroom discussion.

'It's OK, you can get away with that sort of thing in English!'

The introduction of any kind of controversial subject matter into the classroom will initially destabilize the status quo, as students assimilate this change and attempt to see whether it gives them any new power. Despite our cherished autonomy within the classroom, it is vital both for us and for students to appreciate that what goes on in our lessons is always viewed in the context of the wider school. In schools operating anti-racist and anti-sexist policies, it is usually clear enough from their constitution how an individual breach is to be treated. A good policy tends to lay down relevant areas of responsibility and indicate the accepted procedure for dealing with abuses. However, for the teacher committed to an anti-heterosexist approach on her/his own, it is essential to know what to do about incidents which would, were they racist or sexist, normally result in some kind of referral to the school's pastoral network. If senior colleagues cannot be relied upon to become involved in a disciplinary capacity, then the teacher needs to develop strategies of her/his own to combat unacceptable behaviour. Failure to do this would soon lead to classroom anarchy as students come to realize that they can get away with comments and actions, which, in the normal course of events, would result in some kind of referral.

But disciplinary issues are unlikely to pose the greatest problem which the isolated teacher has to face. Due to the prevailing climate of public opinion regarding the introduction of lesbian and gay issues into the curriculum, s/he will have to face the very real chance of there being parental complaints, questioning the issue's validity in English lessons. If the head of department and/or the senior management are prepared to offer at least tacit support, then it may be possible to allay their fears and protect the teacher. If, however, no support is available, then it is likely that the issue will be killed off before it ever reaches the stage of provoking parental response. However, were it to get that far, the implications for the teacher's credibility and status, both in the short term and once teacher appraisal is introduced, are indeed frightening.

Resources

Even the lone, enterprising teacher who has managed to straddle the last two hurdles is still far from home. It is all very well deciding to sharpen the focus of English to include an awareness of homophobia but how exactly is this to be done? Although there may not be a substantive body of knowledge which constitutes the essence of English, there are the criteria of exam boards and the impending national curriculum. Ours is a resource-based subject and our main resource is literature. From the primary school through to colleges of further education, the staple diet of students is books. Most of what we teach is rooted in novels, plays and poetry. And, as has been demonstrated so clearly from the experiences of those working towards anti-racist and anti-sexist models of English teaching, the materials with which we present students are of vital importance. With the possible exception of the ideologically dubious *A Taste of Honey*, what books is the isolated teacher likely to have already at her/his disposal? Certainly it is quite feasible to create one's own resources, but time and expense may well mitigate against this. To follow such a path, unresourced, can lead only to a great deal of additional work and the possibility that, without access to appropriate literature, little will be achieved.

Out on a limb: the English department

Obviously the situation will be much improved for an English department working in concert, towards the achievement of an agreed goal. A strong department ought to be able to fend off criticism both within the school and from parents. The promotion of positive images of lesbians and gay men can be written into its aims and objectives and take its rightful place alongside other initiatives. This combined effort will be to take the pressure off individual teachers and allow each to feel supported in what s/he is doing. Resourcing will be easier as, cut-backs aside, it will now be possible to order in relevant materials for the department.

Although the concept of a united department, committed to combating homophobia, is a much more realistic option than an individual teacher ploughing away on her/his own, there are still likely to be difficulties associated with this approach. The first is that it will isolate the department from others within the school. The spin-off from this is the probable marginalization of the issue, resulting in students and other staff perceiving it as an English hobby-horse and of little or no relevance outside the English classroom. However, this is clearly an eventuality which is preferable to doing nothing at all. On a positive level, the stance of the English department could well lead to other areas following suit and, perhaps, to the ultimate adoption of some kind of whole school approach.

In concert

The benefits of a whole school policy are implicit from the foregoing two sections. First, it would depersonalize the issue, bringing it within the ambit of issues which concern the entire school. Second, it would set up agreed procedures, ensuring a unity of response and a coherence of objectives. It would remove accountability from an individual teacher or department and result in the headteacher's having to take clear responsibility for both its representation to parents, governors and the local education authority (LEA) and its implementation within school.

The problem, of course, is to get such a policy into place. There are a small number of schools who currently have policy documents but the vast majority of these were adopted *before* Section 28 became law. In early 1989 a working party at North Westminster Community School in London, which included the school's headteacher, Michael Marland, presented their findings to the rest of the staff. On the basis of their report, they urged them to back a statement which would integrate a policy of anti-homophobic practice throughout the school. Due to staff resistance, much of which ostensibly centred around individual teachers feeling themselves to be inadequately trained to be able to deal with the issues, this failed.

Even were a staff group to be united in its desire to tackle homophobia at a school-wide level, the chances of an institution being brave enough to challenge what most LEAs, parents, governors and almost all newspapers would no doubt (erroneously) see, as the letter of the law must be very slim. This is not to say that it is impossible; a large East London college of further education has recently instituted a supplement to their existing equal opportunities policy, focusing specifically on lesbian and gay issues. It is just that very few institutions chose to adopt sympathetic policies when the political climate was more favourable, thus giving the cynic cause for a certain amount of scepticism as to the possibility of many further developments.

This fear ought not, however, to deter schools from attempting to raise the issue, or even contemplating some form of integrated approach. It may well still be possible in some schools to achieve these goals. However, there is much which can be done short of adopting a policy statement. Many schools and LEAs have 'sneaked' references to sexuality into their anti-sexist initiatives. (Despite the praiseworthy utterances of their apologists, claiming that this was a deliberate, ideological decision because sex-role stereotyping and sexism are two sides of the same coin, it is an almost irresistible temptation to suggest that it was more politic to hide the word 'sexuality' in amongst other words beginning with the same three letters!) The point is better made by looking again at ILEA's own equal opportunity commitment.

> The Inner London Education Authority is committed to achieving an education service which provides equality of opportunity and freedom from discrimination on the grounds of race, sex, class, sexuality, or disability in both education and employment.
>
> (ILEA 1984: 9)

However such words 'sexuality' or 'sexual orientation' come to find their way into policy documents is, in practice, irrelevant. The important matter is that they are there in some form, as this will lead individuals to be able to rely on at least some measure of support. Even in their absence, it might still be possible to gain a favourably wide interpretation of wording which lays down, for example, that the school or LEA is committed to 'equality of opportunity' or is 'opposed to discrimination'. While not imposing a school-wide approach to homophobia, this may allow 'concerned' teachers the freedom to raise the issue and to seek disciplinary action to right its excesses.

I feel that there is little point in looking at the possibility of an LEA-wide policy as Section 28 has effectively put an end to any such new developments. Its provisions are aimed specifically at local authorities and until such time as its interpretation is judicially considered, it is extremely unlikely that an education committee would be permitted, by its political bosses, to test its validity.

The role of parents

> School should be a place where values and beliefs emerging from the home, or conveyed by the media, can be examined, argued about, and reflected on. So, whatever views I hold as a parent, even dearly held ones, I would want them to be up for constructive criticism at school . . .
>
> In the same way, I know that my children already know about my married life-style. An educational curriculum which only reflected this choice about sexuality would seem to affirm my values. But actually it fails to fulfil my educational hopes for my children, because it doesn't give them information they need about real differences that exist in society, and because it doesn't offer them an alternative place to reflect on sexual choices and values . . .
>
> So like all concerned parents, I want my children to make good, mature moral decisions about their sexuality. But they can't do this from a position of ignorance, uninformed gossip or of total dependence on my values. So I welcome the support of

the school, not to reinforce exactly what I think and choose, but to help them reflect carefully on the plural nature of our society, so that they can choose for themselves. (Statement by a Christian mother, submitted to Haringey Council's curriculum working party on lesbian and gay issues in education)

No apology is made for the length of the extract just quoted. It is extremely rare to see, in print, the views of parents which are anything but vehemently opposed to and 'justifiably' fearful of the inclusion of issues of sexuality in schools' curricula. Perhaps the greatest misnomer of the whole debate around Section 28 and the 'promotion' of homosexuality is the unquestioned opposition of parents to the combating of heterosexism and positive images work.

there was a real concern that local authorities were targeting some activities on young people in schools and outside, in an apparent endeavour to glamorise homosexuality. Not unnaturally, parents have become increasingly worried and resentful about public money being used in this way to influence the attitudes and behaviour of impressionable young people.
(The Prime Minister, The Rt Hon. Margaret Thatcher, in a letter dated 3 March 1988 quoted in Stop the Clause Education Group 1989: 18–19)

There is no good reason why parents should necessarily oppose an objective, balanced presentation of issues of sexuality. However, the media campaign which invented and then harangued the 'Gay Lessons' to which children were supposedly being subjected took it for granted that it was speaking on behalf of parents who were both disgusted and surprised by what was ostensibly taking place. This latter assumption was as unfounded as the assertion, made by Dame Jill Knight MP, that 'children under two have access to gay and lesbian books in Lambeth play centres' (Stop the Clause Education Group 1989: 28). As early as 1987 Haringey, who were seen as the main 'culprits', distributed a leaflet, 'Equal Opportunities – what every Parent needs to know about Lesbian and Gay Issues', to *every* household in the borough.

What is clear is that good educational theory and practice requires that parents are involved fully in developments of this kind, both in their initial stages and on a continuing basis to monitor their operation. Schools need to work in partnership and through honest and open negotiation with all those whom they purport to serve. This lesson is shown to excellent effect in the example of one South London comprehensive which has been seen as something of a pioneer in the field of sexuality. A fuller account of its achievements can be found in the very useful *Section 28: A Guide for Schools, Teachers and Governors* (Stop the Clause Education Group 1989).

The role of school governors

As was mentioned in Chapter 1, the Education (No 2) Act 1986 placed responsibility for sex education with school governing bodies who, since September 1988, have been required to make and keep up to date a separate written statement on their school's policy on sex education (Section 18). Schools have therefore had to make conscious decisions as to whether or not to include homosexuality within their sex education curriculum. In theory, this is an important decision because a failure to present relevant issues to the governing body for ratification in their statement would make their subsequent inclusion in the syllabus technically illegal.

> In order to love effectively one must understand and hence it is vital that any good education programme must include some treatment of homosexual relationships alongside any treatment of heterosexual relationships. The nature and content of such a programme will have some mention in the school information booklet which all governing bodies must provide and will in any case become apparent to parents through the medium of homework.
>
> (London Diocesan Board for Schools 1979, quoted in Haringey Education Service 1988: 96)

As with parents, there has been a tendency among more radical workers in education to believe that school governing bodies are constituted solely by people who still rue the demise of Genghis Khan! Certainly there are governors who have seemed disdainful of many contemporary educational developments but, again as is the case with parents, there is no reason why their status automatically furnishes them with reactionary views. Once again, the key seems to be to allow governors an active role in any discussions, canvassing support, ideas and opinions and utilizing the particular skills and expertise which individual members may have to offer. Returning to the example of the South London comprehensive mentioned above, what follows is the text of the motion which the school's governing body passed unanimously, in response to Section 28.

> This governing body expresses its total opposition to Section 28 of the Local Government Act and reaffirms its commitment to the teaching of equal opportunities in this school. We feel that this section will prevent the teaching and learning about the full range of sexuality that exists in society and remove the right of governors, staff and parents to exercise their discretion as to the discussion of such matters in the classroom as appropriate. We also feel that the section will work against the fight against bigotry, discrimination and intolerance. We express our full support for the staff of the school in continuing the excellent work so far achieved in this area.

The role of the pastoral curriculum

> Teachers and pastoral staff should be made to realise that the attitudes of anti-gay pupils/teachers are responsible for the 'problems' concerning being lesbian/gay and that being lesbian/gay is not a problem. (Female, 20)
>
> (Trenchard and Warren 1984: 60)

It is the pastoral network which will have to bear the brunt of any commitment to tackling homophobia in school; whether the level of involvement is just that of an isolated teacher or of the entire staff group, instances of abuse and other conduct of a disciplinary nature will need to be referred. What the pastoral network needs to do is to examine how it intends to respond to this.

The following underlie my own thinking on this subject.

a) Homosexuality is just as natural and normal for the homosexual as heterosexuality is for the heterosexual.
b) Homosexual relationships are intrinsically just as capable of good or bad as heterosexual relationships.
c) Homosexuality is not an illness; homophobia . . . is.

(Jackson 1987: 74)

It could be argued that this, or some similar statement of principle, needs to inform the provisions of the pastoral curriculum in so far as they relate to homosexuality. Failure to adopt a theoretical approach will result in there being little possibility of any action being taken or, if it is taken, will provide its opponents with the opportunity to challenge it. It is vital that there be some ideological rationale for any decisions reached and the resulting sanctions imposed, if these are not then to be open to question and criticism. Once this issue has been discussed, the next step is to decide whether the pastoral care offered is to take the form of a *passive* or an *active* kind.

The *passive strategy* is designed to plaster over an uneven system rather than reconstruct that system, as the active approach seeks to do. The former entails providing lists of useful addresses and contacts, such as Lesbian and Gay Switchboard, local youth groups and Parents Enquiry, and making these accessible. Whether these are posted on a noticeboard, or are to be available from pastoral staff only on request, will depend on the stance taken by the individual school. If the latter course is adopted, then staff involved will have to endeavour to create an atmosphere of trust in which students will be able to disclose their 'dark' secret. They will need to be completely certain that what they say will be treated in absolute confidence and that their wishes, with regard to their families' not knowning, are totally respected. This must also extend to any records which are kept by the school. Sex education and preventive HIV education will need to be presented in a practical rather than a sensationalist or 'moral' manner. This approach, while not as comprehensive or far-reaching as the active model, would certainly be an improvement on what is currently on offer in most schools.

The *active strategy* involves actually dealing with the issue before it presents itself as a 'problem'. It requires a much more arduous and committed involvement from the staff involved and, probably, can become operative only after much in-service training. To be successful, lesbian and gay staff would need to feel secure enough to come out and thus provide the first stage in the process of the 'normalization' of homosexuality. Students, beginning to consider their own sexuality, would then have the opportunity to seek advice and information from others, whose understanding could be guaranteed. Perhaps the distinction being drawn here is between those capable of empathy and those capable of, at best, sympathy.

For the lesbian or gay, of whatever age, the first person to whom they describe their feelings is likely to have a huge influence on their subsequent development. A negative reaction may create problems which could take years to work through. Talking to someone for the first time needs to be recognized as the massive step which it undoubtedly is and one which all lesbians and gay men always remember. Many put it off until a favourable response is a near certainty, or until desperation leaves them no choice but to speak. Some will be so scared of the reactions of others that they will never come out to anyone. The only hope of breaking this debilitating circuit of silence and misery is by creating a situation in which students have nothing to fear from the person they tell. This point is more fully developed in the discussion of the rights and responsibilities of lesbian and gay teachers.

The active approach concentrates on the perpetrator of homophobic abuse, rather than its victim. As has been said before, the emphasis must be on preventing 'queer-bashing', not curing 'queers'. If the pastoral system honestly accepts that it is homophobia, not homosexuality, which is the illness, then it has no choice but to commit itself to countering *that* illness. To that end, punishing students for manifesting fervent homophobic abuse is of little use, if that is the only course of action taken. It is, after all, these people who need help. It is simply no good, as has often been the case with anti-racist and anti-sexist initiatives, to establish a new policy and then focus on counselling and helping only those suffering from its breach. That type of approach can never defeat the problem, it is merely a palliative measure, which is of little real help except, perhaps, to the conscience. Therefore, pastoral staff will need to counsel individuals and discuss their misconceptions with them, if they are ever to appreciate why what they did is considered wrong. Otherwise, there will be no qualitative difference for them between being referred for calling a fellow student a pansy and failing to produce a piece of homework.

A point to bear in mind, in relation to either strategy, is that staff need carefully to consider their legal position: two males who are having a sexual relationship, where one or both of them is under 21, are both guilty of a criminal offence. Anyone who knows of this and does not report it can be guilty of withholding information from the police or of aiding and abetting, if they offer any advice which furthers such a relationship. Students would obviously need to feel confidence in the 'discretion' of staff, so as not to risk court appearances.

Rights and responsibilities of lesbian and gay teachers

In some circumstances and in some contexts [a teacher coming out] could amount to the promotion of homosexuality.

(Howard 1987)

This previously quoted opinion, although apparently unsound from a legal perspective, does however echo a popular belief; that of the innappropriateness of a teacher disclosing her/his sexuality. This section concentrates on the extremely complex issue of whether lesbian and gay teachers ought to come out. It examines the reasons why they might choose to do so, the arguments against such actions and the impact upon students (and staff) of there being an 'out' teacher.

'I don't want to whisper anymore'

It is impossible to quantify the number of teachers who are open with their students about their homosexuality, but the existence of such varied organizations as Lesbians in Education, Feminist Lesbians in Education, Gay Men in Education, Lesbian and Gay Workers in Education and the National Association of Teachers in Further and Higher Education Lesbian and Gay Group (amongst others) is sufficient evidence that there are some. What follows is an attempt to try to put into perspective why anyone would choose to place their job on the line and come out of the closet.

The importance of being honest

I still wasn't entirely happy, not entirely myself. I was dressing 'straight', trying to behave 'straight' and constantly conscious of surpressing a crucial part of my lifestyle, myself, me. As a result, I was less happy, and I believe now, a less effective teacher.

(Lena, 'I don't want to whisper anymore', in City of
Leicester Teachers' Association 1987)

One of the major stumbling blocks in any discussion relating to sexuality is the almost universal misconception that the word is some kind of shorthand for sex. For a young man to be described as heterosexual is in no way inconsistent with his being a virgin. (It is just unlikely that he would ever admit it!) So, if it can be accepted that sexuality is not just (or even directly) about its first three letters and is, in fact, far more concerned with an individual's life-style and personal identity, then it becomes easier to understand why so many lesbians and gay men accord it such a primacy in their lives. Often, even the 'right-on' heterosexual, will ask why it is necessary always to harp on about sexuality. S/he will no doubt grant that prejudice and discrimination exist but will still be at a loss to see why it is such a major issue. If s/he were to step back and evaluate quite how much of her/his daily conversation and behaviour was permeated with confirmation of and references to her/his own sexuality, then the question might begin to seem as facile to the questioner as it must to its recipient. Husband, wife, wedding ring, kids, anniversaries, in-laws, boy/girl friend: all are the currency of everyday social intercourse for the heterosexual. Yet if the lesbian or the gay man has the temerity to mention her/his sexuality, let alone the existence of a partner, then s/he is immediately accused of forcing the issue down other people's throats.

But sexuality *is* about a great deal more than bed. It encompasses types of belief, conduct and attitude. People who share the same sexuality and gender are likely to have more in common with one another than with those who don't. (This may well have much to do with conditioning, stereotyping and other sociological factors, but it also involves large components of shared experience and a similarity of outlook.) To subsume this would, for the heterosexual, be completely untenable, yet it is what society currently demands of 10 per cent of its population. The emotional strain of being forced to hive off what is, for all of us, a major part of our identity, without even considering the impact of feeling the need to pretend to be something or someone else, is a huge disability imposed on lesbians and gay men.

And it is no different for teachers. Some would even argue that it is actually worse, in that honesty and trust ostensibly constitute such a large part of the stuff and substance of our current methodolgy. A History teacher might mention a castle he visited with his wife and two daughters, but his colleague, who teaches Art, would be hard pushed to talk so openly about an exhibition she saw with her female partner and the latter's son. Yet neither is being indiscreet or overt, nor doing much more than sharing a commonplace with students. Neither is discussing sex, nor proselytizing. But one is deemed to be acceptable, while the other is held to be unnecessary and invalid.

The lesbian or gay teacher who decides to be open about her/his sexuality is only saying, 'this is an aspect of my life which is important to me and I have *chosen* to be honest and share it with you'. No more than that. It is as much an invitation to discuss sex as the History teacher's revelations concerning his family. Nor is it an attempt to win converts, even if that were possible. It is, on the one hand, a purely descriptive statement, saying nothing more than does a wedding ring, while on the other, it is a recognition of the importance of being honest.

Positive images

The teacher who decides to come out at school often does so, not only for her/his own benefit or peace of mind, but also for what s/he perceives to be the benefit of students. More than anyone, s/he is aware of the pressures and problems which face the lesbian or gay teenager, as most will remember their own school experiences, specifically those relating to sexuality. Given that it is unlikely that such lesbian and gay teachers will have fared particularly well while they themselves were students, many are subsequently influenced in their decision to come out by the impact which they hope it will have on their own students.

In discussing the role of the pastoral curriculum, it was suggested that the active approach, in order for it to be successful, needs lesbian and gay staff to feel secure and comfortable enough to be able to come out. The reason why this was deemed necessary was so that those students, who are beginning to consider their own sexuality, have the opportunity to seek advice and information from others, whose understanding can be guaranteed.

If teachers could be openly gay and under no threat, not only could they give a positive image of homosexuality, they could also impart support and information. (Female, 19)

Perhaps it would be easier if gay teachers were more open about themselves (pigs might fly!) and a much more extensive and comprehensive sex education including gay lifestyles. (Male, 18)

Lesbians teachers, whether they are out or closetted, are helpful as role-models, implicit support etc. (Female, 17)

(Warren 1984: 19)

These quotations exemplify the practical applications of a positive role-model as a 'sympathetic ear' for the lesbian or gay teenager, while extending its ambit to include the recognition of the need for such positive images to demonstrate to them the potential both for survival and success. Obviously it is important for them to see happy, well-adjusted, successful lesbians and gay men getting on with their lives. For most it will be something of a revelation, as they, like their heterosexual peers, will have derived their views about homosexuality from society at large and the media.

> Gay people have none of the benefits of being brought up by fellow-members of their minority. Members of other minorities may have unpleasant lessons to learn, but at least Jewish children learn about Hanukkah before holocaust, Passover before pogrom. Homosexuals . . . are poorly placed to rebut even the most preposterous description of homosexuality. 'This isn't true of me', many gay people may think, 'but perhaps it is true of the majority of my minority. How can I know?' When a book called *Queens* . . . appeared a few years ago, Gay Switchboard received a number of distress calls from people who wanted to know if the book was accurate, in which case they proposed to end it all. Is there another minority that genuinely wouldn't know the difference between an accurate portrait and a piece of sensationalist fantasy?
>
> (Mars-Jones 1987)

The lesbian or gay teenager will eventually have to discover that fantasies are not reliable or representative, if s/he is to come to terms with her/his sexuality. Yet no such pressure exists for the heterosexual teenager and s/he will be at liberty to continue in her/his belief in the veracity of such fantasies until confronted with a real-life situation, involving a homosexual. For some, this may never happen and they will go to their graves believing homosexuals only ever appear in newspapers or television programmes. Others may anchor their views and actions in such misconceptions, and treat those that they encounter on the basis of these misconceptions.

Where the young people's quotations (Warren 1984) need expansion, however, is that they limit the benefits of positive images to lesbian and gay students. Yet they are only part of the picture. The existence of an openly lesbian or gay teacher can provide *all* students with an approachable foil to the stereotypical images of lesbians and gay men, giving them the opportunity to weigh their received knowledge against their own experience. They will be confronted by a person, busily involved in the day-to-day business of her/his chosen career. A well-balanced, happy person who incidentally has relationships with other people of the same sex. In one word, normal. After all, what else ought there to be to say about lesbians and gay men?

The 'political' perspective

The central thesis of this book rests on the belief that homophobia is a set of attitudes whose direct result is the repression of a sizeable section of the population. One of the major spin-offs of any type of repression is that it engenders a concomitant reaction, an opposition. As was documented in Chapter 1, in the lesbian and gay communities this opposition crystallized at the time of the Wolfenden Report (1957) and has grown in strength and voice since then. What are perceived as discriminatory laws and practices have taken homosexuality out of the privacy of individuals' lives and transferred it to the public domain; the personal becoming the political. The Sexual Offences Act, 1967, Section 28, civil wrangles over custody, inheritance and the provision of appropriate health care have all ensured that the life-styles and identities of lesbians and gay men are now issues of public concern and legal regulation.

The corresponding result of this governmental intervention, and the opposition to it, has been a politicization of many lesbians and gay men. This has not always followed strict party lines but has tended instead to concentrate on the fight against oppression, with support being vested in whichever party seems most prepared to join the fight or, in practice, is least hostile to it. Central to this politicization has been the realization that sexuality itself can be, and often is, a political issue. Many lesbians will argue that they come to their lesbianism as a conscious, political decision as feminists. The decision to come out can have extremely strong political connotations. The courageous stance taken by the actor, Ian McKellen, to come out in 1988 was motivated by his abhorrence of what Section 28 intended, particularly in the sphere of the arts, and his desire to prevent its implementation, by adding his (famous) name to the fight.

For teachers too, coming out can have a political dimension. Apart from the desire to be honest and the conviction that it is important for students to experience positive images of lesbians and gay men, both of which can be seen as political in themselves, the teacher, contemplating coming out, is also likely to be motivated by two, more overt, considerations. The first is a will to challenge bigotry and the second, of a much broader nature, is the opportunity which it provides to attempt to change social attitudes as they relate to homosexuality.

In terms of challenging bigotry, the lesbian or gay teacher will seek to confront individual manifestations of prejudice which will no doubt be exhibited, as a result of her/his coming out. This can take the form of a direct response to unacceptable comments and behaviour, as well as the almost subliminal erosion of stereotypical beliefs through day-to-day interaction. As to trying to alter society's attitudes to homosexuality, s/he might well seek to contextualize homophobia within the galaxy of prejudice, in addition to demonstrating its potency and destructiveness. This is in no sense to peddle a party political line of any kind. It is merely an attempt to put homophobia in its logical place and to describe its inevitable outcomes. If students remain unaware of the results of their actions and beliefs, there is precious little incentive for them to re-evaluate and modify them.

'Keep your voice down, there are children around'

As might be expected, there are a range of arguments which have been levelled against those described above, attempting to dissuade the lesbian or gay teacher from coming out. Not all of these are pure negations or homophobic knee-jerk reactions; some are firmly rooted in the belief that school is not the appropriate place for sexuality to be discussed.

Students are too young to understand

This first line of argument suggests that aspects of sexuality are too complicated to be fully understood by school students. It postulates that the complexity, inherent in the diversity of human sexual and emotional behaviour, is so great as to elicit only the most simplistic response from children. Further, it argues that they will be unable to place such sexual behaviour within the context of an emotional and moral framework and will, instead, be tempted to conduct 'homosexual' experiments. Nowhere is this particular argument better expressed, than in the following example.

The DES Circular, *Sex Education at School* (DES 1988a), allows schools to 'present facts in an objective and balanced manner so as to enable students to comprehend the range of sexual attitudes and behaviour in present day society'. In response to this, the Revd Peter Mullen wrote

> This amounts to a licence to teach perversions. And who is able to draw the line between describing and explaining on the one hand and advocacy on the other? Certainly not impressionable teenagers whose curosity about erotic sexual practices has been fired by teachers too zealous in explaining 'the range of sexual attitudes and behaviour'.
>
> (Mullen 1987: 22)

The argument as presented is underpinned by the scientifically unfounded theory that children go through a homosexual phase which most then outgrow. Based upon this, it then makes several erroneous assumptions. The first is that the word 'children' is taken to describe an homogenous group, which possesses a uniformity of intellectual faculties and experiences. Second, it ignores the fact that students, in the late twentieth century, will have pre-existing knowledge and opinions about homosexuality. Finally, it falls into the trap of believing that heterosexuality is so fragile and tenuous a state that it is threatened by the very mention of an alternative. What it signally fails to acknowledge is that school places students within a highly complex social structure, characterized by constantly shifting group dynamics and internal power struggles. Its ultimate sanction is peer ostracism. In addition, two of the worst insults which can be levelled at one of their number are 'poof' and 'lezzie'. Is Peter Mullen really saying that students will be quite prepared to flout their own beliefs and orientation, the opinions of family and friends and risk their standing within school, merely because a teacher has mentioned same-sex relationships?

Proselytizing

Interwoven with the argument that children are too young to cope with issues of sexuality is the belief that the lesbian or gay teacher comes out only in order to win converts to the cause. Even if there were any truth in this, as was described during the examination of the provisions of Section 28 in Chapter 1, it is extremely improbable that sexuality is as transferable as a railway ticket.

It is impossible to estimate whether there are, in fact, any lesbian and gay teachers who do seek to proselytize. (The head of Religious Education at a boy's secondary school in Birmingham, who was sacked over claims that he had 'encouraged' homosexuality, was recently awarded £12,000 in compensation for unfair dismissal: *The Pink Paper*, 14 October 1989.) All that can be said is that quite why they would undertake such a task is difficult to appreciate. Homosexuality is hardly a comprehensive belief system of the same type as, say, Roman Catholicism and yet Catholic teachers, in non-denominational schools, are never accused of attempting to use their positions to win disciples, despite the fact that their faith actively advises them so to do.

As to the baser purposes, purported to be the hidden agenda of homosexuality, Ken Livingstone (speaking in the House of Commons on 15 December 1987) said that in the thirteen years of his involvement with ILEA, *every* known instance of sexual abuse in schools related to girls and young women assaulted by heterosexual, male teachers. Bigots can also be directed to a report produced by the Catholic Social Welfare Committee, *An Introduction to the Pastoral Care of Homosexual People*, which states, 'In fact, it would seem proportionately to their numbers in the population, that heterosexuals are more prone to child molestation than homosexuals' (quoted in Haringey Education Service 1988: 90–1).

Why are you bringing your personal life to school?

One of the most common objections raised against the teacher who intends to come out is that it is unnecessary. It is argued that what s/he does in her/his private life is private and is an inappropriate matter to bring into school. Once again, there is the confusion between the words sex and sexuality. It is totally correct that a teacher's sex life is of no relevance to students. The difference here is that sexuality has no direct relation to sex. A man may view himself as gay throughout his life and yet choose never to have sex with anyone. He is, in no sense, any *less* gay than someone who has had an active physical relationship with his lover of thirty years' standing.

Heterosexuals advertise their sexuality whenever they wear wedding rings or talk of spouses, children and their relationships. To come out is actually no more than to say 'I lead a different kind of life-style'. By implication, it suggests that the speaker has the potential for a different form of sexual expression from the accepted norm, but only the same way that to declare oneself to be an orthodox Hasidic Jew equally pertains to sex.

Wider benefits of coming out at school

As was indicated above, the teacher, considering coming out at school, may well feel it incumbent upon her/him to do so not only for personal reasons, but also because of those benefits which s/he believes others will gain from such an action. Basically, these fall into categories: those advantages intended for students and those accruing to other members of staff.

For the good of students
One boy stayed behind after school one day and told me that he was gay. I was the first person he'd ever told. He said that he'd told me because he'd known me for four years and known that I was gay all that time – I'd been out all that time – and he could see that I'd survived. That's very important for gay pupils, that they see gay teachers surviving. For me it was very moving, though I found it a huge responsibility as well. I just wish that I'd had a gay teacher when I was at school. (Secondary school teacher)

If teachers could be openly gay and under no threat, not only could they give a positive image of homosexuality, they could also impart support and information. (Female, 19)

(Warren 1984: 34)

These two quotations draw a distinction between the effects of being taught by an out teacher for lesbian and gay students and that for their heterosexual peers. This area was covered, above, in the section dealing with the reasons why a teacher might choose to come out, from which the second quotation is taken. In essence it argued that lesbian and gay students would have a sympathetic ear; and also that they, in common with all students, would see a positive image of a happy, successful lesbian or gay man.

For the good of colleagues
Having an out gay teacher created a greater awareness of the prejudices and misconceptions held by staff and pupils. It provided a legitimate opportunity to ask questions and get information. It certainly helped me to realise how much hostility exists towards gay people and how little the subject is dealt with in the curriculum.
(Ghulam Sarawari, secondary school teacher in London, in Gay Teachers' Group 1987: 81)

This quotation indicates the effects on colleagues of there being an out teacher within school. First, it will force those others to adopt a stance; ideally through discussion. As a result, information, advice and mutual fears can be voiced, rescuing the issue from the grasp of internecine gossip and providing an opportunity in which all staff will actively have to consider homosexuality and, in so doing, confront their own prejudices. Such a situation can act only as a catalyst, creating that awareness of prejudice of which Sarawari speaks. It is a pessimistic observation, but one which may well be true, that seeing one of their 'own' suffer, may well invoke the sympathy of many more teachers than would be the case were the problems solely encountered by a student. Second, once the issue has been raised through a teacher having come out, it will be difficult then not to formulate, at the very least, a concerted staff response to homophobic behaviour. While falling short of a whole-school policy, it will none the less protect both the individual teacher and students at risk from acute homophobia. It has tended to be the case that schools have ignored the issue of sexuality, until the point at which a teacher coming out makes it impossible to ignore any longer. In the present climate, it does appear that it is up to individual lesbians and gay men to place the issue on the school agenda.

The purpose of this chapter has been to examine the role of staff in any opening up of the issue of sexuality in school. It is all very well to suggest that sexuality is an area which ought to be dealt with in the curriculum, but it becomes essential, due to its 'sensitive' nature, to ensure the levels of support which will be offered and the personal risks involved, before so doing. To that end, the chapter looked first at the position of the individual, concerned teacher, then the committed department and finally at the possibilities of a school-wide approach. The importance of the pastoral curriculum was then discussed and the remaining part of the chapter dealt with the heated, but vital, issue of whether or not lesbian and gay staff should come out.

8 Where to from here?

In the introduction to this book, I posed a number of questions whose purpose was to challenge its very existence. Why has this book, whose central theme is the place of sexuality within the English curriculum, been written at this particular time? What possible relevance can this issue have to the teaching of English or, for that matter, education in general?

In attempting to answer these questions, I submitted that the task of this book was four-fold. First, it had to examine how and why it is that sexuality has come to find itself centre-stage in both the educational and political debate. Second, it needed to make a convincing case for the inclusion of lesbian and gay issues in schools. Third, it had to assess the implications of such a policy for the teacher of English. Fourth, it should suggest possible materials, approaches and strategies in order to achieve this end.

The political perspective

Like it or not, the issue of sexuality is now firmly established as both a potential subject of everyday discussion and an item on the political agenda. The combination of the discovery of HIV-related illnesses, the radical policies of a small number of Labour-controlled local authorities and the need to implement more concrete proposals for the teaching of sex education, have all led to homosexuality becoming 'big news'. Nowhere has the debate been more vociferous and more acrimonious than in relation to its place within schools' curricula.

There appear to be three main reasons for the intensity with which this debate has raged. Firstly, opponents of proposals whose aim is to defuse homophobia hold the belief that a child's sexuality is so fragile that the presentation of anything short of utter contempt for – or, better, an outright dismissal of – homosexuality is likely to create such a temptation that either it will result in youngsters being persuaded either to experiment in homosexual sex or it will cause them to choose to become fully fledged lesbians and gay men themselves. This argument, relying on the capacity of individuals to swap and choose sexualities rather like trading stamps, takes no cognizance of the fact that there is no evidence whatsoever to confirm the view that sexuality is quite so transferable. No one has, as yet, been able to prove what factors are operative in influencing sexual orientation; whether it is a matter of nature or nurture or a mixture of both. Equally, there is no evidence to give credence to any explanation as to why, if a free choice exists, anyone would ever choose to enrol on a minority group so unpopular, so vilified and so discriminated against that, only a few years ago, psychiatrists and psychoanalysts were able to amass a great deal of money offering 'cures' to those unable to cope with its attendant pressures.

The second great fear brought on by raising the issue of sexuality with students is that because homosexuality is seen by many to be morally, religiously or biologically 'wrong', it is unimportant and inappropriate to tackle the prejudice which follows in its wake. Instead, words like evil, unnatural and abnormal are used to dismiss homosexuality. It is of no account that it affects 10 per cent of the population, irrespective of race, sex, religion or class. As a result, it is viewed as a sickness and, calls are made not for tolerance but for an effective cure. This is clearly a difficult set of arguments to counter, depending as they do on beliefs and attitudes which are not particularly susceptible to empirical evidence and pure logic. The only injunctions which can be offered up against their potency are hard facts and appeals to that humanity which first influenced and is supposed still to permeate those faiths.

The final fear, ignited by the desire to include aspects of sexuality in schools, is based on the belief that the real reason why teachers want to raise such issues is motivated by nothing so innocuous as pure politics but is in fact much darker. Rather than seeking to dispel prejudice as they claim, what lesbians and gay men are really hoping to achieve is the seduction of those in their charge. All the available figures show this to be so much fiction; yet in many ways the gay man as child molester is one of the most pervasive stereotypes promulgated by our heterosexist society.

As was suggested in Chapter 1, the primary piece of legislation in this area, Section 28, actually has had very little substantive effect to date. Its main result and, many would argue, its primary intention is to induce a climate of self-regulation. Its provisions are so vague that local authorities and, by implication, individual schools have become so fearful of prosecution that they veto proposals which would in no way break the letter of the law. However, the spirit of the legislation was always made quite clear and there is little doubt that a reactionary judge would find few difficulties in upholding a complaint of the Section's breach, by applying a 'generous' interpretation of its extremely nebulous, woolly wording.

Even today, with the Section firmly in place, homosexuality is still a live political issue. Both the Green Party and the Social and Liberal Democrats have commitments to lesbian and gay rights. The Labour Party, in the light of an amendment passed at its conference in October 1989, is under much pressure to extend its own, somewhat bland, rhetoric to include the abolition of the Section and the lowering of the inequitable age of consent for gay men at least to 18, albeit still a full two years higher than that for heterosexuals. Although not yet as powerful a lobby as those in the USA, British politicians are coming to realize the importance of securing the lesbian and gay vote, at a time where few parties are in a position to alienate any statistically significant electoral minority.

In addition, the continuing AIDS crisis has forced politicians to address issues of sexuality and sexual behaviour. In so doing they have had to liaise with lesbian and gay organizations, whose swift response to HIV has saved, and continues to save, many lives and whose practices and information resources still lead the field in preventive health education, infection and disease management, and intensive care. The recent Health Education Authority advertising campaign in the lesbian and gay press has clearly demonstrated even the current British government's willingness to shelve politics and party dogma and accept a partnership with the lesbian and gay communities, making use of the greater resources which they have to offer.

The social perspective

Of the four tasks which I set myself at the outset, it is perhaps the discussion of what I call the social perspective of homosexuality which is the most important. It is all very well examining how issues of sexuality have come to the fore both socially and politically, the pedagogic justifications for their inclusion within the school curriculum and the methods through which this might be achieved, yet all this will be of little persuasive weight if it has not first been shown that such a policy is both necessary and urgent.

The harm which is currently inflicted upon lesbian and gay youngsters was documented in Chapter 2. The London Gay Teenage Group research (Trenchard and Warren 1984) is invaluable in uncovering the scale of the misery and damage wrought and is *still* the only such piece of work in existence. Ploughing through its depressing statistics, it is difficult to refute its claims that the current education system is, at the very least, guilty of denying access to the curriculum to some 10 per cent of our students. At its worst, the ethos which we all tolerate continues to foster a climate of violence and ostracism in relation to that 10 per cent.

And none of this takes any account of the loss and misinformation which is the lot of those other students who have not, and will not later, come to identify themselves as lesbian or gay. No one is an island. Few of us could successfully maintain that we are not part of a society, a community and a family, however we may feel about each of them. Whatever our own sexual orientation, it is unrealistic to go through life, hoping that homosexuality will somehow go away, that it has no bearing on our own lives.

An old Gay Liberation slogan of the early 1970s proclaimed 'WE ARE EVERYWHERE!' and it still has much truth in it. One-tenth of all the people we know, in whatever sphere of our lives (whether they are friends, colleagues or family), is likely to be lesbian or gay, however certain we may be in our assumptions of their heterosexuality. One-third of all lesbians are mothers; many gay men are fathers. One in ten parents will produce a lesbian or gay child. Homosexuality *is* a fact of life.

To continue to ignore the relevance and importance of homosexuality in both the overt and covert school curriculum is to continue to allow the misery which lesbian and gay students currently suffer. It is to stand back with the certain knowledge that thousands will experience violence and bullying, will under-achieve, will even contemplate and sometimes attempt suicide. And all because those in charge of society's morals, and many teachers themselves, have taken it upon themselves to exclude the experiences of and deny basic rights to those whose only 'crime' is their difference.

The pedagogic perspective

In Chapter 3 I set out to examine the relevance and amenability the teaching of English to a policy whose purpose is the integration of issues of sexuality within its ambit. To that end, I focused upon three main areas. First, looking at the broad aims of English, it was argued that these already include a commitment to the personal, social and moral development of students, under which such a policy would hardly be inappropriate. I discussed how students themselves perceive English, as evidenced by the limited amount of research which has been undertaken, and contended that it too laid great emphasis upon the importance of students' own contributions and personal experiences. Finally, I presented a close examination of how ILEA has 'sold' its anti-racist and anti-sexist policies to English departments and what lessons these provide for an initiative designed to defuse homophobia.

It was then my intention to draw out from these three main areas, possible implications for sexuality. These were identified as the knowledge and the experiences which students bring to English, a critical examination of the materials which we use, the need to recognize the dual nature of discrimination, in which both the aggressor and her/his 'victim' require equal consideration and, finally, the fact that it is essential that an integrated approach to the issue is adopted, rather than consigning it to a part of a unit or a topic which is then superseded by the next.

It is hoped that what all this has demonstrated is the very appropriateness of English as an important site for issue-based curriculum development and, specifically, its potential for this particular issue. It was argued that English should 'encompass the whole spectrum of human experience' and that to hive off homosexuality is to make a mockery of that statement. If we really value the experiences and opinions of the students whom we teach, it is patently untenable effectively to ignore the validity of many of the contributions which 10 per cent of those students seek to offer.

The practical perspective

For the hard-pressed teacher of English, currently drowning in a sea of documentation relating to the national curriculum and assessment and the like, an appeal to further modify existing practice is unlikely to meet with unmitigated jubilation, however s/he might feel about the issues raised by such an appeal. We are already under far too much pressure to initiate curriculum development lightly. Therefore this book would be of little practical use unless it featured, alongside its more theoretical and academic passages, concrete suggestions and schemes of work which could, with a minimum of alteration, be used at the classroom chalk-face.

For this reason, Chapter 4 dealt with the nuts-and-bolts of contemporary English teaching, as well as any possible changes which might be required when the national curriculum fully comes into operation. As a result of that 'initiative's' stated aims for secondary English, I included a discussion of the place of Drama and Media Studies in this context, as well as examining the roles of primary, secondary and further education. The concentration on secondary schools is deliberate, appearing to me to be the most appropriate sphere in which to open up the issue effectively to the largest possible number of receptive students.

Chapters 5 and 6 were each devoted to the case study of a novel around which teachers might decide to base a unit of work. Notwithstanding the fact that each may have its faults, they ought to provide the concerned teacher with, at the very least, the bare bones upon which to flesh out a course of lessons to combat heterosexism. In a sense, they are included merely as examples of the amenability of the teaching of English to the issue. No doubt, there are better schemes and more appropriate books. Yet the two schema which have been included are, to the best of my knowledge, the only available published resources. It is to be hoped that the ideas and suggestions they contain will be improved and extended, as more teachers take up the issue and more books are used. (The appendix, which follows this chapter, features as annotated list of other possible suitable literature.)

As was stated in the preface, I have become increasingly angered that it has been necessary to publish such a book in 1990. In so many other spheres, our pedagogic theory has completely outgrown the vapid Victorian soil in which the state education system was hastily rooted. Yet we are still at the stage at which most of us need to be persuaded *not* to oppress a sizeable minority of those whom we teach.

In writing this concluding chapter, I hope that the book has answered the questions it posed (and raised several new ones). As was also indicated in the preface, apart from its subject-matter and a time difference of some thirty years, there is, in many ways, little to distinguish this book from those urging teachers to try to integrate issues of race into the curriculum in the 1950s. (Fifteen years later, it then became the turn of gender.) Throughout its course, I have strived to maintain this link with such arguments, not only to provide the book with a sense of cohesion and to make its own arguments more appealing to those convinced first time round, but also because it is my firm belief that whatever the particular prejudice being discussed, each manifestation is inextricably intertwined with all of the others by a deep-rooted desire to gain and then maintain power and privilege over those deemed to be a threat.

The centrepiece of this book has been to present a convincing argument in favour of some kind of positive action within English teaching to defuse homophobia. I firmly believe that it is the last 'great' area of prejudice which must be tackled. However, unlike the other 'isms', it is the most personal, given the fact that those in charge of educational policy, those who have espoused policies of anti-racism and anti-sexism, have rarely been Black or women. However, 10 per cent of them are lesbian or gay and even to raise the issue is viewed by many people as a personal declaration of homosexuality. Therefore any discussion tends to centre around the proclivities of individuals seen to show concern and the main question, how best to combat oppression, is submerged in a swirling sea of moral censure. No clearer example of this need be found than the parliamentary by-election of 1983 in Bermondsey and the disgusting treatment meted out by the media (and his own party) to the Labour Party candidate, Peter Tatchell.

But, clearly, something must be done. At present, we are consigning 10 per cent of students in our schools to misery. They experience problems of isolation, ostracism and verbal and physical abuse. One in fifty of the students whom we teach will attempt suicide as a direct result of problems related to their sexuality. Of the London Gay Teenage Group research sample, 25 per cent had been referred either to a doctor or a psychiatrist; 21 per cent had been beaten up; 17 per cent had come into contact with the police because of their sexuality; 11 per cent had been thrown out of home (Trenchard and Warren 1984). These statistics make unpleasant and depressing reading, especially when viewed with the certain knowledge that many (if not all) of them could be avoided. And that teachers have both the opportunity and the power to achieve this.

So we find ourselves in the situation where many who believe in the importance of this issue none the less feel themselves to be impotent and are unable to persuade others of the vital need for immediate action, in case it leads those others to presume that these advocates of reform are, in actual fact, the very people whom they fear! This vicious circle must be broken and those of us, committed to irradicating this invidious inequality, have no choice but to fight for change and damn the misinformed prejudices of others.

In today's political climate, where we are exhorted to 'return to Victorian values', where Section 28 was enacted to ossify oppression and the AIDS crisis has been cynically manipulated to lend a hand, where government ministers feel it politic to speak quite openly about the laxity of the law as it relates to homosexuality; if that all-pervasive closet, which society seeks to strengthen further, is not finally razed and used for firewood, it will be bolted so securely that no one will ever be able to get out.

Appendix

What now follows is an annotated list of materials which teachers of English might find useful when resourcing work based around the issue of sexuality. The books appear under five headings:

- novels with a lesbian theme
- novels with a gay theme
- short stories
- drama
- poetry.

Autobiographies, biographies, histories and sociological and political texts have been excluded, due to the limited scope of this book. The lists themselves are in no way intended to be either prescriptive or exhaustive but it is hoped that they will provide sufficient materials from which to start.

As with all literature used with students, it is suggested that any material from the lists is previewed first, especially as some of it contains sections which might be considered to be sexually explicit. The age suitabilities, which follow each annotation, are no more than approximate suggestions; the individual teacher is by far the best person to gauge the abilities and receptiveness of her/his students.

Many of the entries are taken from ILEA's excellent (now out-of-print) *Positive Images: A Resources Guide for Teaching about Homosexuality, including Lesbian and Gay Literature for Use in the Library and the Classroom*, Materiography no. 11 (ILEA 1986a), which is used here with the kind permission of ILEA. Those entries which are taken or substantially derived from that materiography are indicated by an asterisk*.

Novels with a lesbian theme

Allarde, Jeaninne *
Legende: The Story of Phillipa and Aurelia
Alyson, 1984
Phillipa becomes 'Phillip' and marries Aurelia. The story is based on a legend, still told in Brittany, of two women who loved each other and lived, together with their adopted daughter, happily for twelve years. **14+**

Alther, Lisa   *
Other Women
Penguin, 1985
Easy to read, this adult novel focuses on Hannah, a therapist, and Caroline, a lesbian client. It is interesting and moving and has much to say about life in middle-class America in the 1980s.   16+ and staff

Bayliss, Sarah   *
Vila: An Adventure Story
Brilliance Books, 1984
This is the story of Nina and Masha, two 15-year-olds who have nothing but arranged marriages and child-bearing to look forward to in their village in Dark Age Russia. Their adventures, through their encounters with Vila, a fortress huntress and teacher of skills as yet unknown to the young women, are told in an accessible and lively manner. The book contains lots of ideas about feminism, anarchy and co-operation and portrays the close love and friendship between the two young women.   14+

Brady, Maureen   *
Folly
Crossing Press, 1983
This book tells the story of the development of a lesbian relationship between a Black woman and a white working-class woman in a Carolina mill town, painting vividly the difficulties they face in a society imbued with both racism and heterosexism.   15+

Bratenburg, Gerd
What Comes Naturally
The Women's Press, 1986
An hilarious account of growing up in Oslo in the 1960s, addressed to a hypothetical man who is tied to a chair and forced to listen. The novel hits out hard at traditional assumptions of 'normal' and 'abnormal'.   15+

Brown, Rita Mae   *
Rubyfruit Jungle
Corgi, 1978
A lively and funny account of an American girl growing up and becoming a lesbian. Her attempts at heterosexuality and the prejudices which she faces are clearly described. A positive book which is in places sexually explicit and marred by its anti-Semitism.   14+

Brown, Rita Mae   *
Six of One
Corgi, 1980
This moving and highly entertaining novel charts the lives of six women, their families and friends in the small town of Runnymede, USA. It is both funny and serious and written in a clear and easily accessible style.   14+

Clausen, Jan
Sinking, Stealing
The Women's Press, 1985
Josie, an adult, and Erika, who is 10, are both runaways. Rhea, Erika's mother and Josie's lover, has been killed and Erika's father has gained legal custody. The story is about their

struggle to maintain a parent–child relationship in the face of the father's opposition and society's total refusal to recognize any legal or social bond between them.   16+

Fairbanks, Zoe *
Benefits
Virago, 1979
This novel is set in the not-too-distant future, where women's fertility is controlled by the state through a 'social benefits' system and eventually by enforced contraception. That is until the women organize to change things. This exciting and deeply moving novel opens up a wide range of questions around social and personal control of sexuality and fertility, while remaining an exciting read.   15+

Gallford, Ellen *
Moll Cutpurse: Her True History
Stramullion, 1984
A lively and entertaining novel telling the story of the life and loves of a lesbian pickpocket, acrobat and fighter for the rights of women in Elizabethan England. Based on the true story of Mary Frith, it is a splendid celebration of a piece of history many would like to hide and of the rarely documented strength of women.   15+

Garden, Nancy
Annie on my Mind
Farrar, Straus & Giroux, 1982
(See Chapter 6)   14+

Gearhart, Sally *
The Wanderground
The Women's Press, 1985
The Wanderground provides a Utopian vision of the future in which the Earth has rebelled against the rule of men and their misuse of the environment. The women have re-established their relationship with Nature when all is threatened by the men's desire to regain control. This is an exciting account of the women's battle to retain their new-found life-style and freedom.   15+

Geller, Ruth *
Triangles
Crossing Press, 1984
A refreshing story where being in a lesbian relationship is not seen as in any way being a problem, even when it becomes stormy. Sunny is more concerned about being Jewish and the anti-Semitism that she faces. She and her family are well portrayed, particularly her energetic grandmother, Rose. An interesting and positive book that raises several important issues.   16+

Guy, Rosa
Ruby
Gollancz, 1981
Ruy, 18, has moved from the West Indies to Harlem. She has to cope with her father's strictness and the antipathy of her classmates. Finally, she forms a friendship with one of them, Daphne, which deepens into a relationship. However, due to her fear of her father and the differences between their values, the relationship ends. It is a moving novel which is often funny.   15+

Hautzig, Deborah *
Hey Dollface
Fontana, 1979
Well-written account of two American schoolgirls who fall in love with each other. The book charts both the girls' reaction to the development of their sexuality and their original confusion clearly and with great sensitivity.   14+

Hayes, Penny
The Long Trail
Naiad, 1986
Schoolteacher Blanche and dance-hall girl Teresa discover an unthinkable love. But the year is 1869 and their love cannot be tolerated by the mores of the 'pioneering west' so they flee – this is the story of their journey and their love.   15+

Klein, Norma
Breaking Up
Pan Horizons, 1986
While visiting her father and stepmother in California, Alison not only falls in love for the first time, with her brother's (male) best friend, but also learns that her mother and her neighbour, Peggy, are lovers. For this reason, Alison's father is trying to gain custody of the children. The portrayal of Alison's mother and Peggy is very sympathetic and positive. Alison's struggle to come to terms with the range of human relationships which she encounters is described in a simple, enjoyable manner.   14+

Knudson, R. R. *
Fox Running
Avon, 1985
The story of two young women runners from very different social and racial backgrounds and their struggles to reach the top. An exciting story that shows the strength of women and the need for interpersonal support and co-operation.   14+

Knudson, R. R. *
You are the Rain
Dell, 1978
Powerful story about a group of young women on a canoeing trip in the Florida Everglades. Presents very positive images of the young women as individuals and the power of collective action.   14+

Livia, Anna *
Relatively Norma
Onlywomen Press, 1982
Hilarious account of a visit by Minnie, radical lesbian feminist from Brixton, to her mother in Australia. It's not difficult to read, although the absence of speech marks may be off-putting. An entertaining novel.   15+

Lorde, Audre *
Zami: A New Spelling of my Name
Sheba, 1984
A vivid moving account of a young Black girl growing up in Harlem in the 1930s and as a 'gay-girl' in Greenwich Village in the 1950s; it explores lesbian loves and life-styles and her search for a Black identity.   15+

Lynn, Elizabeth A.
The Northern Girl
Arrow Books, 1987
A book for fantasy enthusiasts. It is set in a society in which same-sex relationships are accepted with a calm matter-of-factness. Sorren, the northern girl of the title, journeys north to try to understand her roots. 15+

Manning, Rosemary *
The Chinese Garden
Brilliance Books, 1984
The Chinese garden is a small, secret garden at the heart of the grounds of a boarding school where Rachel is a pupil in the late 1920s. It is also a metaphor for Rachel's developing sexuality and is a refuge from the coldness and restrictions of the school. While not an easy book, it well repays the reader for staying with it. 16+

March, Caeia
Three Ply Yarn
The Women's Press, 1986
The story of three British women with interwoven lives. Accessible and often very funny. The book opens with an excellent description of working-class lesbian life in the 1950s. However, the novel is sexually explicit in places. 16+

Miller, Isabel *
Patience and Sarah
The Women's Press, 1979
The romantic and heroic story of two women who fall in love and dedicate their lives to each other, based on the true story of two women who lived in the USA in the nineteenth century. It is told by the two women, alternating as narrators, and the reader is very quickly involved with their lives and their viewpoints as the novel develops. 15+

Namjoshi, Suniti *
The Conversations of Cow
The Women's Press, 1985
This short and simply written novel draws equally on Hindu mythology and practice as well as lesbian feminist politics to give an incisive, witty and original view of the way women relate to each other and to men in a heterosexist society. Bhadravati is the Brahmin lesbian cow of the title, who is also a goddess who manifests herself in many forms, trying the patience and expanding the consciousness of Suniti, a lesbian separatist. 15+

Piercy, Marge *
Braided Lives
Penguin, 1982
In this story of women growing up in the USA in the 1950s, Piercy recreates the tensions and fears that lie beneath the surface. Funny, angry and entertaining, she writes of the Women's Movement and explores love and friendship between women. 16+

Piercy, Marge *
Woman on the Edge of Time
The Women's Press, 1978
Conni Ramos is a 37-year-old Mexican-American whose life has been worn out by the brutality of racism and sexism and the practices of an uncaring and overworked psychiatric

profession. Having been chosen for a 'research project' at the hospital in which she has been forcibly held, she discovers that she is also a 'catcher' and can travel into the future. Her version of the Utopia she discovers there encourages her to seize power to act in the here and now. This is a beautifully written, frightening and thought-provoking book.   16+

Rule, Jane
After the Fire
Pandora, 1989
The story traces the impact on the lives of a number of the island's inhabitants of a fire which kills Dickie, a drunk and 'laddish' local. Red, a fiercely independent young woman, is carrying Dickie's child and is determined, despite the views of others, to have it. Karen, a lesbian running away from a failed relationship, now leads a closeted life, but is none the less drawn into the web spun by the fire and the enigma that is Red.   15+

Rule, Jane
Desert of the Heart
Pandora, 1986
The novel upon which Donna Deitch's excellent film, *Desert Hearts*, is based. It is set in the early 1960s. Evelyn goes to Nevada to get a divorce and meets Ann Childs, a hedonistic rebel to Evelyn's staid respectability. The story tells of their growing relationship.   16+

Rule, Jane
Memory Board
Pandora, 1987
This is the moving story of Diana, a doctor, and her lover of forty years, Constance, who has senile dementia. Diana's brother, David, enters into their environment and finds himself more at home with them than he does with his conventional nuclear family. It is a poignant story, dealing with the twilight world of dementia and a love which transcends youthful, corporeal 'perfection'.   15+

Rule, Jane
This is Not for You
Pandora, 1987
Kate watches her friends confront issues of sexuality, marriage, work and wealth. She worships one of them, Esther, but cannot bring herself to love her openly. She has brief relationships with other women but these never detract from her love for Esther, the woman she can never bring herself to share her life with.   16+

Russ, Joanna *
The Female Male
The Women's Press, 1975
A recognized science fiction classic, Joanna Russ's novel has been described as an 'interplanetary exploration of feminist inner space' and tells the stories of four women from different worlds and different times whose lives become woven together. Despite a somewhat complex structure, this book is both an entertaining and moving read, charting the growth of these women and all our potential futures.   16+

Scoppertone, Sandra *
Happy Endings are All Alike
Dell, 1978
An excellent novel which deals with the developing lesbian relationship between two

16-year-old women and the reactions of those around them. The book explores the relationship in a sensitive and engaging manner. However, a rather graphic rape scene at the centre of the book needs to be carefully handled and may preclude the book's use with young men.   **14+**

Severance, Jane *
Lots of Mommies
Lollipop Power, 1983
This American book tells of Emily, a child who lives with her mother and two other women, and her first day at school. Although the lesbianism is not made explicit, the child is laughed at by her peers for her family situation. However, the book does end on a positive note and is a rare example of a book for younger schoolchildren presenting a lesbian family. Illustrated with line drawings. Also suitable for discussion with older children.   **7–10**

Taylor, Sheila Ortiz *
Faultline
The Women's Press, 1982
This is the hilarious account of a lesbian mother who lives with her lover and their children, a Black gay male child-minder and 300 rabbits! Simply told, the novel is a celebration of human diversity and makes an excellent and undemanding read.   **14+**

Walker, Alice *
The Color Purple
The Women's Press, 1983
This touching, complex, Pulitzer-prize-winning novel is the story of two Black sisters living in the harsh, segregated world of the deep South between the wars. Celie confides her feelings to God about her situation as a woman 'given' in marriage to Albert, merely to look after his children, while her sister Nettie writes to her from Africa about her life. Through Shug Avery, a singer, Celie discovers the love and support of women and finally rediscovers Nettie and hope. An absorbing, beautifully written novel, it celebrates the liberation of Black women together in a moving, direct way.   **15+**

Wilson, Barbara Ellen *
Murder in the Collective
The Women's Press, 1984
Two print collectives, one left-wing and one radical lesbian, are about to merge when a murder takes place. A wonderful, political whodunnit which opens up issues of racism and traditional left politics as well as lesbian rights, while remaining a gripping and entertaining story.   **15+**

Wings, Mary
She Came Too Late
The Women's Press, 1986
A fast-moving whodunnit in the Chandler tradition, focusing on Emma Victor, who works for the Women's Hotline. It is an urbane study of lesbian sexuality and the games people play.   **16+**

Winterson, Jeanette
Oranges are Not the Only Fruit
Pandora, 1985
This semi-autobiographical story tells of a Catholic schoolgirl with an extremely doctri-

naire mother. The story charts her growth, sensitively but with much humour, following her life as she falls in love with a cashier at the local supermarket.   15+

Novels with a gay male theme

Baldwin, James *
Just Above my Head
Dell, 1980
Arthur Montana, a successful Black American blues singer, is discovered at the opening of the book lying dead in the basement of an English pub. The rest of the book is the story of how he got there. It is also the story of his family and friends. One of James Baldwin's best novels, it presents one of the few positive literary pictures of a successful Black gay man readily available in Britain.   15+

Bosche, Susanne
Jenny Lives with Eric and Martin
Gay Men's Press, 1983
The *enfant terrible* of positive image books, this book portrays a day in the life of Jenny, a young girl, who lives with her father and his gay lover. It is presented in photo-text format and makes no issue of the situation it portrays. Given its format, it seems to be intended for an age group who may well be incapable of grasping its meaning. However, it hardly deserves its reputation as the lesbian and gay *Kama Sutra!* Probably unsuitable for classroom use.

Carson, Michael
Sucking Sherbert Lemons
Black Swan, 1989
The story of Benson, a fat 14-year-old, inspired with equal amounts of fervour for Catholicism and his peers' bodies. He enters a seminary but finds the temptations of the flesh as potent as they were in the outside world. He leaves St Finbar's and befriends the sixth-form's star pupil. The book is somewhat graphic, but never pornographic, and is extremely funny.   16+

Chambers, Aiden *
Dance on my Grave
Pan, 1982
The sensitively told and amusing story of a 16-year-old's discovery of his sexuality when he finds himself falling in love with another boy. Through a dazzling range of literary styles, the book charts his growth from confusion to confidence in his sexuality as the relationship develops. Despite the death of one of the leading characters, the book is both positive and lively.   15+

Ecker, B. A. *
Independence Day
Avon, 1983
Mike gradually realizes that he is attracted to his best friend, Todd, but feels certain that Todd does not feel the same way. The story realistically charts the difficulties created by Mike's growing awareness of his sexuality and his eventual coming out to Todd and his own family. A positive book that is also an entertaining read.   15+

Ferro, Robert
The Family of Max Desir
Arena, 1987
The story of Max and the conflict his love for Nick causes to his Italian-American family, which he equally loves. The novel tells of Max's exile from the family due to his iron-willed father. His eventual return is caused by the sadness brought on by the fatal illness of Max's mother. A fairly complex book but one which is none the less highly enjoyable. **16+**

Forster, E. M.
Maurice
Penguin, 1975
Forster's classic novel, published posthumously; it tells of Maurice's journey from a pillar of respectability to the student at Cambridge who begins a relationship with Clive. The pressures of Edwardian morality prove too great for Clive, who is able to 'rediscover' an attraction to women. Despite the fact that, to modern eyes, the story is not as positive as it might be, it is none the less both a classic of its time and the testament of a major literary figure sentenced to silence. **16+**

Fox, John *
The Boys on the Rock
Arena, 1985
The story of a 16-year-old American boy who becomes aware of his gayness in the late 1960s. He falls in love and begins a relationship only to discover that not everyone is as positive about their gayness as he is. Simply written, this entertaining story gives an accurate account of growing up and discovering one's sexuality. However, it may be considered by some to be too sexually explicit. . **15+**

Hall, Lynn *
Sticks and Stones
Dell, 1972
A 16-year-old boy forms a friendship with an older man whom he later discovers to be gay. This information also quickly travels around the small American village in which they both live and the young man soon learns the awful power of prejudice and gossip. This book tells simply of the effects of such prejudice on all concerned and the young man's struggle to come to terms with the situation in which he finds himself. **14+**

Hansen, J. *
The Man Everybody was Afraid of
Granada, 1984
One of a series of exciting and thoroughly gripping stories with Dave Brandsetter, as an openly gay private investigator, in the central role. Sadly, Hansen's female characters are never drawn as positively as his male ones, but this story is his best all-round work in this field. A good, light read. **15+**

Holland, Isabell *
The Man Without a Face
Dell, 1980
This curious, well-written book tells of the relationship that develops between Justin, the man without the face of the title, and Charles, a 14-year-old boy. The subject is handled with great discretion. **14+**

Ireland, Timothy
The Novice
Gay Men's Press, 1988
The story of Donovan Crowther, 22 and still a virgin, who is drawn to London in his search for love. Told through the unreliable eyes of Donovan, it is the story of innocence and experience and the hopes and realities of first love.   15+

Ireland, Timothy
Who Lies Inside
Gay Men's Press, 1984
(See Chapter 5)   15+

Isherwood, Christopher *
A Single Man
Magnum, 1978
Isherwood's classic novel about the life of a gay Englishman living in California celebrates with humour and sensitivity a homosexual relationship brought to a close by the untimely death of one of the partners and the loneliness of the surviving partner. Yet the book remains a tribute to the resilience of the human spirit and is universal in its appeal. It would make an excellent classroom text.   15+

Jones, Rhodri
Different Friends
André Deutsch, 1987
A deliberately 'right on' book in which all the main characters hail from different ethnic backgrounds. Not just content with this, Jones also adds a barrage of topical social and political issues into this story of the reaction of Chris to learning that Azhar is gay. Despite its almost laboured 'right on-ness', it does little to deflate macho stereotypes and is not greatly recommended.   14+

Leavitt, David
The Lost Language of Cranes
Penguin, 1987
A story of hidden feelings and obsessions. Philip wants to tell his parents that he is gay but worries that it may destroy their already tenuous marriage. Owen, his father, is himself gay but has yet fully to admit it to himself. The exploded secrets leave the family shattered. A well-constructed book, although marred slightly by an unevenness, especially in its characterization.   16+

Martin, Kenneth
Aubade
Gay Men's Press, 1989
A new edition of a gay classic. Written when the author was just 17, it tells of a teenager's first gay love affair.   15+

Maugham, Robin
Wrong People
Gay Men's Press, 1986
A gripping thriller which also deals sensitively with gay relationships. First published in 1967, it tells of Arnold Turner, an English schoolteacher, on holiday in Tangier,

Morocco, and his meeting with wealthy, Anglo-American expatriate, Ewing Baird, whose interest and influence on Turner becomes increasingly sinister.   **15+**

Maupin, Armistead
Tales of the City
More Tales of the City
Further Tales of the City
Babycakes
Significant Others
Sure of You
Black Swan, 1976–90
A series of six bitterly funny novels set around the inhabitants of 28 Barbary Lane, a bizarre household in San Francisco. The landlady, Mrs Anne Madrigal, presides over her 'family' which, in turn, consists of a variety of different 'representatives' of Bay society, including Michael 'Mouse' Tolliver, a gay man whose life-story is one of the constant features within the series. Mrs Madrigal's secret is but one of hundreds of surprises with which the reader is greeted. The novels manage to steer clear of ever being too sexually explicit, yet retain their huge humour.   **16+**

Nelson, C.   *
The Boy who Picked the Bullets Up
Avon, 1982
An interesting novel, told in letter form, concerning a gay medic in Vietnam. The horrors of war are graphically portrayed as are the sexual exploits of the soldiers. This is an excellent read with much to say about the American presence in Vietnam and the obscenity of war.   **16+**

Payne, Simon
The Beat
Gay Men's Press, 1985
The story tells of a young man who enjoys 'queer-bashing'. One night he visits a local gay haunt, but things don't turn out the way he planned. He himself is beaten to death by a group of men. The remainder of the book examines each of them, focusing on their lives and their involvement in the murder.   **15+**

Rees, David
The Hunger
Gay Men's Press, 1986
Set in Ireland in the 1840s, against a background of turmoil and a potato famine, the novel tells of an English landowner and an Irish peasant farmer. The story deals with their struggles to keep both themselves and their love for each other alive in a society and an era that condemns their acquaintance, let alone their love.   **15+**

Rees, David   *
In the Tent
Dobson, 1979
While stranded on a mountainside during a camping expedition, a group of sixth-form boys learn about themselves and each other. Two of the young men are gay and form a relationship. The story is intertwined with the siege of Exeter during the English Civil War. While this may make the novel a little less accessible to some students, it provides an intriguing, added dimension to the plot. It is an entertaining read which would make an excellent text for study.   **15+**

Rees, David
The Milkman's on his Way
Gay Men's Press, 1982
This book, along with *Jenny lives with Eric and Martin*, was used by the government and the media to 'prove' that positive images was, in fact, merely a euphemism for the exposure of children to explicit sexual practices. The story tells of the sexual awakening of Ewan, a 16-year-old boy. He eventually leaves his home town for London. Although a simply written book, it is difficult to rebut accusations of its being too sexually explicit and its tendency to voyeurism. But, as with *Jenny*, it is hardly the evil, proselytizing text which its detractors suggest. Probably unsuitable for classroom use.

Rees, David *
Out of the Winter Gardens
Olive Press, 1984
This is the story of a 16-year-old boy who discovers that his father, who left home several years before, is gay. Despite a somewhat unconvincing maturity on the part of the boy, this is an entertaining novel that raises an important issue.   **15+**

Rees, David *
Quintin's Man
Dobson, 1976
An excellent account of a heterosexual boy's growth to adulthood and sexual maturity. In the course of the novel, he meets a group of young gay men. His reactions, from confusion to acceptance, as he gains confidence in his own sexuality, are carefully charted. A very useful book for raising the issue of male adolescent sexuality (including homosexuality) in the classroom, as well as a great read.   **15+**

Reid, Forest
Young Tom
The Retreat
Uncle Stephen
Gay Men's Press, 1987–9
This beautifully written trilogy charts the childhood of Tom Barber from an 11-year-old boy to a 15-year-old adolescent. Set in late-nineteenth-century rural Ireland, the series is evocative and often magical, containing delightful description of the boyhood of the sensitive and intelligent Tom. Often compared to Proust for his capacity to 'recapture' time long buried in memory, especially in relation to childhood, Reid's books have a shimmering, ephemeral beauty and child-like naivety which recommend them highly.   **15+**

Ridley, Philip
Crocodilia
Brilliance Books, 1988
The excellent story of Dominic Neil, an 18-year-old East End boy who meets and becomes obsessed with Billy Crow, a young punk, living next door. Through Billy, Dominic becomes involved in sex, fantasy, deceit and people with bizarre lives. A hugely entertaining and challenging read but one which some might find a little graphic in its eroticism.   **16+**

Ridley, Philip
In the Eyes of Mr Fury
Penguin, 1989
The book charts the impact of the past on Concord Webster and Webster Martin, lovers whose families have become inextricably intertwined over a number of generations. The atmosphere is one of mysticism and deep secrecy, portrayed alongside Ridley's obsession about time and its legacies. A difficult read but one which repays its reader handsomely.   **16+**

Scoppertone, Sandra *
Trying Hard to Hear You
Bantam, 1981
This book deals with the reaction of a young woman to the discovery that two of her closest friends are gay and have developed a relationship together. It is a convincing and moving account of the way in which anti-gay prejudice creates both personal and social tragedy. Despite the seriousness of its theme, it is a lively and engaging account of the rarely acknowledged problems faced by young people in a heterosexist society. Recommended as a classroom reader.   **14+**

Seabrook, Mike
Unnatural Relations
Gay Men's Press, 1989
This book deals sensitively with the love affair between the emotionally mature Jamie, who is only 15, and Chris, a 19-year-old student. Due to the malice shown to Jamie by his parents, Chris is eventually arrested and tried for 'buggery with a minor'. Despite its great sadness, the book has a positive ending and deals intelligently with the physical aspect of the boys' relationship.   **16+**

Sennett, Richard *
The Frog that Dared to Croak
Faber & Faber, 1982
Tibor Grau, the fictional hero of this novel, becomes an important politician in an Eastern bloc country. He is also a homosexual who has collated notes on his sexual and social development on scraps of paper that make up the body of this work. This entertaining novel is particularly interesting in its depiction of gay life behind the so-called 'Iron Curtain'.   **16+**

Sitkin, Pat
The Alexandros Expedition
Alyson, 1983
A cross between a thriller and a gay love story. Openly gay Hamish and his playboy ex-schoolmate, Evan, set off to rescue a friend who is being held captive by a group of North African fanatics. During the adventure, both men discover much about each other, including the fact that Evan isn't heterosexual after all.   **15+**

Snyder, Anne
The Truth about Alex
Signet, 1981
Brad and his friend Alex are inseparable. Yet Alex is gay and Brad straight. The story charts the impact upon their relationship once rumours begin to circulate at school.   **15+**

Stewart, Leslie
Two of Us
Arlington, 1988
The story of the friendship and subsequent relationship which develops between two teenaged boys. Set in and around a school and dealing, as it does, with the response of teachers and fellow students to the boys, it would make an excellent text for class study. This is the novel based on the controversial BBC film.   15+

Storr, Catherine
Two's Company
Patrick Hardy, 1984
Kathy and Claire are two sisters who, when in France on holiday, meet up with Steve and Val, two young men who attend university together. All seems set for a holiday romance when Claire goes off with Steve and leaves Kathy and Val together. The relationships become complicated when Val comes out as gay and affirms his love for Steve. However, portrayal of all the major characters remains negative and it could well reinforce the notion that homosexuality, not heterosexism, is the problem.   14+

Wakefield, Tom
The Discus Throwers
Gay Men's Press, 1985
The inhabitants of a household above a West London launderette, reacting against the social conventions which have shackled their lives, make various bids for freedom. The results are unexpected, funny and often very moving.   15+

Wakefield, Tom
Mates
Gay Men's Press, 1983
The story of Cyril and Len who meet up during National Service. The novel charts their lives together over the following thirty years in which there are many ups and downs, most as a result of their having to lead closeted existences. A story of survival told with much sensitivity.   15+

White, Edmund
A Boy's Own Story
Picador, 1982
Regarded by some as something of a classic, a sort of gay *Catcher in the Rye*, this story deals with an adolescent boy's handling of his gayness. Unfortunately in this context, it is far too sexually explicit in relation to his sexual experiences for it to be recommended for classroom use.

White, Edmund
The Beautiful Room is Empty
Picador, 1988
The sequel to *A Boy's Own Story*, this follows the narrator through adolescence and into early adulthood. Again, its handling of sex precludes its being suggested as a suitable classroom resource.

Zilinsky, Ursula
The Middle Ground
Gay Men's Press, 1987
The central relationship is between Johannes Von Svestrom, a war-wounded comman-

dant of a Nazi labour camp, and teenager, Tyl Von Pankow, an internee. They meet in a situation which demands that they relate to each other as oppressor and victim, yet they also find themselves reminded of feelings and memories of another relationship where each loved another man. **15+**

Short stories

As with all collections of short stories, each story should be judged individually, therefore no specific age range has been suggested.

Adzaluda, Gloria and Moraga, Cherrie (eds) *
This Bridge Called my Back: Writings by Radical Women of Color
Kitchen Tabel: Women of Color Press, 1983
This anthology sets out to define some of the feminist/anti-racist struggles of a range of Black women in the USA. Using poetry, short story and fiction this inspiring book is a powerful indictment of racism, sexism and heterosexism.

Aurey, Stephen (ed.) *
Messer Rondo and Other Stories by Gay Men
Gay Men's Press, 1983
This wide ranging collection has several that are suitable for use with young people, particularly the title novella. This tells of two 12 year old boys who are frequently bullied at school and, through a newspaper article, find a common cause with gay people. This then leads them into several adventures. Some of the other stories are, however, sexually explicit.

Birtha, Becky
Lovers' Choice
The Women's Press, 1988
A compelling collection of stories focusing on the world of Black lesbians, covering a wide range of experience, from the loss of the lifetime partner of an older lesbian to the discovery by a 14-year-old tomboy that there are grown-up women like her.

Bradshaw, Jan and Hemings, Mary (eds) *
Girls Next Door: Lesbian Feminist Stories
The Women's Press, 1985
This collection of lesbian feminist short stories covers a wide range of experiences and life-styles from Ancient Greece to the twenty-first century. Most of the stories are written in an easily accessible style and several would be appropriate for classroom use.

Clausen, Jan
Mother, Sister, Daughter, Lover
The Women's Press, 1980
Nine beautifully written stories dealing around the subject matter of the title. The intricate web of lesbian relationships is a constant theme. 'Daddy' is particularly recommended.

Dimple, Richard (ed.) *
Cracks in the Image
Gay Men's Press, 1981
Written by and about gay men, this collection presents a range of images of gay men's lives in a variety of styles. Several would be suitable for young people but some are fairly inaccessible.

Elliot, Jeffrey (ed.) *
Kindred Spirits
Alyson, 1984
This collection of science fiction stories by lesbians and gay men contains a wide variety of pieces about the future and of other worlds from writers of varying experiences and abilities. Joanna Russ contributes her beautiful love story, 'When it Changed' which would be suitable for **14+**.

Forbes, Caroline *
The Needle on Full
Onlywomen Press, 1985
A fine collection of science fiction stories which range through time and space from extra-terrestrial beings in a housewife's backyard to two women embarking on a twenty-year journey into space. The structure of several of the stories is quite complex.

Jurrist, Charles (ed.)
Shadows of Love: American Gay Fiction
St Martin's Press, 1989
An absorbing collection of short stories from a number of US writers, most of whom are unknown in Britain.

Kleinberg, Seymour (ed.) *
The Other Persuasion
Picador, 1978
This is a remarkable collection of classic short stories which deal with lesbian and gay life-styles written by such diverse people as Proust, Stein, Faulkner and Forster. It contains works of great style, talent and wit.

Leavitt, David *
Family Dancing
Warner Books, 1985
This collection of short stories charts the pains and occasional pleasures of family life in middle-class USA. Although in no sense about homosexuality, the stories include several positively drawn lesbians and gay characters. This is a compassionate and moving book.

Maitland, Sara *
Telling Tales
Journeyman Press, 1983
The stories in this collection range from Greek mythology to the present, from South America to China and from creation to clinical death. An admirable addition to feminist literature.

Mars-Jones, Adam (ed.) *
Mae West is Dead: Recent Lesbian and Gay Fiction
Faber & Faber, 1983
An excellent collection from Britain and the USA with contributions from Jan Clausen, Jane Rule, Sara Maitland and many others. A recommended teachers' resource.

Mohin, Lillian and Shulman, Sheila (eds) *
The Reach and Other Stories
Onlywomen Press, 1984
This collection of lesbian feminist fiction contains a wide variety of stories. All of

the collection is of a high literary standard and is an absorbing read. Particularly recommended are 'The kestrels' and 'Old photographs'.

Ream, Joseph (ed.)
In the Life: A Black Gay Anthology
Alyson, 1986
A collection of writings in prose and verse by twenty-nine Black gay men about how it is to be both Black and gay in the USA.

Rees, David
Flux
Third House, 1988
A selection of original stories, focusing on aspects of gay love. Some of the stories are, however, sexually explicit.

Rees, David, and Robins, Peter (eds)
Oranges and lemons: Stories by Gay Men
Third House, 1987
Sixteen original short stories by gay men. While some are sexually explicit, there are several which could be used with students. Particularly recommended is 'Nothing like' by Rodney Mills.

Robins, Peter (ed.)
The Freezer Counter: Stories by Gay Men
Third House, 1989
A new collection of short stories by some of Britain's best and most promising gay writers. Strangely enough, it is the Tom Wakefield story which is the only one without a gay protagonist.

Robins, Peter
Summer Shorts
Third House, 1987
A collection of short stories containing much wit and nostalgia, some of which might well be of use with students.

Smith, Barbara (ed.) *
Home Girls: A Black Feminist Anthology
Kitchen Table: Women of Color Press, 1983
With its American origins, this exciting anthology has much to say to and about Black women throughout the western world. Comprising poems, short stories and essays, it has a section on Black lesbians.

Wakefield, Tom *
Drifters
Gay Men's Press, 1984
This collection tells of the lives of a number of gay men, trying to live in a heterosexist world. While all are well written, several are sexually explicit. However, the final story, 'A bit of shrapnel', is a simply written and deeply moving account of the reactions of a young man's family to learning that he is gay.

Drama

Daniels, Sarah
Neaptide
Methuen, 1986
Using the myth of Demeter and Persephone as a starting point, the play, set in 1980s London, traces the interlocking stories of Val, Claire and Diane. Val, who is Claire's married sister, is in hospital waiting 'to recover enough of my sanity to be allowed back to the world that drove me mad'. Claire is a lesbian teacher who is trying to gain custody of her daughter, while Diane is a pupil who refuses to keep her lesbianism hidden at school.

Davis, Jill (ed.)
Lesbian Plays
Methuen, 1987
Four plays exploring lesbian identity from different perspectives. *Any Woman Can* (1973), about coming out; *Chiaroscuro* (1986) deals with awareness of racial identity in addition to sexuality, *Double Vision* (1982) concerns the influence of class and politics on personal relationships, and *The Rug of Identity* (1987) is a lesbian comedy of manners.

Gems, Pam
Queen Christina
In *Plays by Women*, Volume 5
Methuen, 1986
Based on the life of Queen Christina of Sweden who, in the seventeenth century, was brought up as a man to rule the country and then told to marry and breed. Her love for her maid, her abdication and her unsuccessful relationships with men are encapsulated in this forceful drama.

Green, Maro and Griffin, Caroline
More
In *Plays by Women*, Volume 6
Methuen, 1987
Through a stark pantomime, the difficult subjects of anorexia and agoraphobia are explored with originality and daring.

Greig, Noel *
Poppies
Gay Men's Press, 1983
This play deals with the relationship between gay men and militarism and how it is necessary to take a stand against the nuclear state.

Greig, Noel and Griffiths, Drew *
Two Gay Sweatshop Plays: 'As Time Goes By' and 'The Dear Love of Comrades'
Gay Men's Press, 1981
These two interesting and stimulating plays deal with aspects of gay male history. The first, *As Time Goes By* gives an account of gay male oppression and resistance from the Victorian era through Germany in the 1930s to the Stonewall riots in the New York of 1969. *The Dear Love of Comrades* is described in *Gay Sweatshop: Four Plays and a Company*.

Mitchell, Julian *
Another Country
Amber Lane Press, 1982
Taking a public school in the 1930s as a microcosm of society as a whole, this play
examines the ostracism of two senior pupils, one gay, the other a communist, by the rest of
the school. It is now internationally renowned as a film.

Osment, Michael, ed.
Gay Sweatshop: Four Plays and a Company
Methuen, 1989
As well as a detailed and excellent account of the company's comparatively long and
auspicious career, four plays are also included. *The Dear Love of Comrades* tells of the life of
Edward Carpenter, gay socialist and writer, *Compromised Immunity* is a piece about AIDS;
Twice Over, the only contribution from a woman, handles attitudes to lesbians with much
wit and tenderness and; *This Island's Mine* focuses on the twin oppressions facing a Black
British gay man.

Rudet, Jacqueline
Basin
In *Black Plays* edited by Yvonne Brewster
Methuen, 1987
This is a short, uncompromising and pithy play about three Black women's friendships,
two of them lovers, in urban Britain today.

Sherman, Martin *
Bent
Amber Lane Press, 1979
A powerful play dealing with the internment and extermination of gay men during the
1930s and 1940s by the Nazis. There is, however, one scene which is somewhat sexually
explicit, but see Chapter 5 for the play's selective inclusion.

Wandor, Michelle (ed.) *
Strike While the Iron is Hot
Journeyman Press, 1980
A collection of three plays on issues of sexual politics by three socialist/feminist theatre
companies. Particularly recommended is *Care and Control* from Women's Gay Sweatshop,
which deals with the difficulties that several women, including a lesbian couple, have in
obtaining custody of their children. All three plays are entertaining, easy to stage and raise
many points for discussion.

Wilcox, Michael (ed.) *
Gay Plays *
Methuen, 1984
A collection of plays with gay male themes, set between the 1930s and the present.
Although all are interesting, *Submariners* has been shown on BBC television and is
probably the most useful for raising discussion.

Poetry

Burford, Barbara, Macrae, Lindsay and Paskin, Sylvia (ed.)
Dancing the Tightrope: New Love Poems by Women
The Women's Press, 1987
An anthology professing to explore aspects of women's sexual love. It draws on a wide range of cultures and backgrounds and includes heterosexual, as well as lesbian, poetry.

16+

Burford, Barbara, Pearse, Gabriela, Nichols, Grace and Kay, Jackie
A dangerous knowing: Four Black woman poets
Sheba, 1984
The first collection of poetry written by four Black, British-based women. Their work reflects the depth and complexity of their lives, covering many different themes. **16+**

Cavafy, C. P. *
Collected Poems
Edited by George Savidis
Hogarth Press, 1984
A new translation of the works of the Greek poet who lived between 1863 and 1933. Cavafy is seen as probably the most original and influential Greek poet of this century. The poems contain humour, political cynicism and frankness. **16+**

Cooke, Stephen (ed.) *
The Penguin Book of Homosexual Verse
Penguin, 1983
A collection of lesbian and gay poetry from ancient Greece to the present day which includes the work of famous poets whose homosexuality has been ignored. It mistakenly (and foolishly) includes twenty-five homophobic limericks and several misogynist poems by gay men. It is therefore useful only as a resource work for the teacher.

Duffy, Maureen *
Evesong
Sappho, 1985
These are powerful and poignant poems. **15+**

Grahn, Judy *
The Works of a Common Woman
Onlywomen Press, 1985
Introduced by Adrienne Rich, these poems date between 1946 and 1977. The collection contains pieces on a wide variety of different subject matter. **16+**

Griffin, Caroline
Passion is Everywhere Appropriate
Onlywomen Press, 1989
A selection of lesbian feminist poetry, by a London English teacher, dealing with ordinary, contemporary British life as it affects lesbians, but focusing particularly on love. There are many fine pieces in this volume, many of which may be of use with students. **16+**

Hacker, Marilyn
Love, Death and the Changing of the Seasons
Onlywomen Press, 1987
Sonnets telling the passionate story of the love affair between two women, from meeting to parting. It is, in effect, a graphically detailed novel written in verse. It is often somewhat sexually explicit.   **16+**

Halliday, Caroline
Some Truth – Some Change
Onlywomen Press, 1983
A collection of poetry which examines the politics, the loves, the career and the connectedness of its lesbian feminist poet.   **16+**

Jin, Meiling *
Gifts from my Grandmother
Sheba, 1985
This collection charts the life of a lesbian of Chinese lineage, living in Britain. She comments in a clear and direct way on a wide range of issues which are important to her: migration, racism, pollution and nuclear war, as well as celebrating emotional and physical relationships between women.   **15+**

Lorde, Audre *
The Black Unicorn
W. W. Norton, 1979
In this collection, Audre Lorde explores what it is to be a Black woman, a mother, a daughter, a lesbian and a feminist in the USA today. Her poetry documents, in a clear and accessible way, the all too rarely heard voice of a Black, working-class lesbian.   **16+**

McEwen, Christine (ed.)
Naming the Waves: Contemporary Lesbian Poetry
Virago, 1988
Poems from both sides of the Atlantic with contributions from more than seventy poets. The poems cover a huge canvas of experience and perception but all are 'part of the same endeavour, the telling of important truths'.   **15+**

Mohin, Lillian (ed.)
Beautiful Barbarians: Lesbian Feminist Poetry
Onlywomen Press, 1986
Britain's first lesbian feminist anthology. Using a variety of literary styles, these poems describe and redefine lesbian experience.   **16+**

Mohin, Lillian (ed.)
One Foot on the Mountain: An Anthology of British Feminist Poetry, 1969–79 *
Onlywomen Press, 1979
An anthology designed to combat the assumption that heterosexuality is the norm for women. 'Lesbian play on TV' is particularly useful for initiating discussion on media images of lesbians. Some of the poems are, however, pretentious.   **15+**

Namjoshi, Suniti and Handscombe, Gillian
Flesh and Paper
Jezebel Tapes and Books, 1986
The poems form a dialogue between the two women who write to, for and with each other

as friends, poets, lesbians and lovers. This is unique in the sense of equality and partnership present throughout the sequence. **16+**

Parker, Pat *
Movements in Black
Crossing Press, 1983
The poetry of a Black, working-class lesbian living in contemporary USA. Many of the poems speak with power and clarity and there is much that is suitable for use in the classroom, although some of the language may be unsuitable for younger pupils. **14+**

Rich, Adrienne *
Fact of a Doorframe: Poems Selected and New, 1950–84
Norton, 1985
Prefaced by a useful introduction by Rich, the poems embrace continuity and change over the past thirty years. Amongst many other varied experiences, it documents her struggles as a lesbian in the Women's Movement and her work in both the anti-racist and anti-sexist lobbies. **16+**

Sappho *
Poems and Fragments; Translated and with an Introduction from Josephine Balmer
Brilliance Books, 1984
A new translation with a lengthy and useful introduction putting Sappho, the lesbian poet who lived in the sixth century BC, into historical and critical context. **14+**

Attention is also drawn to selected poems by W. H. Auden, Allen Ginsberg, Thom Gunn, A. E. Housman, Walt Whitman and Oscar Wilde.

Bibliography

Allen, J., Kerr, L., Rolph, A., and Chadwick, M. (compilers) (1989). *Out on the Shelves: Lesbian Books into Libraries*, London, Association of Assistant Librarians.

Altman, D., Vance, C., Vicinus, M., Weeks, J., and others (1989). *Which HOMO-SEXUALITY? Essays from the International Scientific Conference on Lesbian and Gay Studies*, London, Gay Men's Press.

Alyson, S. (1985). *Young, Gay and Proud*, Boston, Alyson Publications.

Anonymous (1989). 'Miss is a lesbian: the experiences of a white lesbian teacher in a boys' school', in H. De Lyon and M. F. Widdowson (eds) *Women Teachers*, Milton Keynes, Open University Press, originally published in *Teaching London Kids*, 1985, 23.

Armitage, G., Dickey, J. and Sharples, S. (1987). *Out of the Gutter: A Survey of the Treatment of Homosexuality by the Press*, London, Campaign for Press and Broadcasting Freedom.

Arnold, R. (ed.) (1983). *Timely Voices: English Teaching in the Eighties*, Oxford University Press.

Austin-Ward, B. (1986). 'English, English teaching and English teachers: the perceptions of 16-year-olds', *Educational Research*, 28, 1, 32–42.

Babuscio, J. (1976). *We Speak for Ourselves: Experiences in Homosexual Counselling*, London, SPCK.

Baker, M. (1984). *Gays in Education*, PGCE dissertation, Institute of Education, London.

Barnes, D., Barnes, D. and Clarke, S. (1984). *Versions of English*, London, Heinemann Educational.

Bazalgette, C. (1989). *Primary Media Education: A Curriculum Statement*, London, British Film Institute Education Department.

Bergler, E. (1956) *Homosexuality: Disease or Way of Life*, New York, Hill and Wang.

Bolton, G. (1984). *Drama as Education: An Argument for Placing Drama at the Centre of the Curriculum*, London, Longman.

——(1986). *Selected Writings on Drama in Education*, ed. D. Davis and C. Lawrence, London, Longman.

Burbidge, M. and Walters, J. (eds) (1981). *Breaking the Silence: Gay Teenagers Speak for Themselves*, Joint Council for Gay Teenagers.

Campaign for Homosexual Equality (1978). *Homosexuality: A Fact of Life*, London, Campaign for Homosexual Equality.

Cant, B. and Hemmings, S. (1987). *Radical Records: Thirty Years of Lesbian and Gay History*, London, Routledge.

Central Advisory Council for England (1967). *Children and their Primary Schools*, London, Report of the Central Advisory Council for England.

City of Leicester Teachers' Association (1987). *Outlaws in the Classroom; Lesbians and Gays in the School System*, City of Leicester Teachers' Association (NUT).

——(1988). *Challenging Oppression: Lesbians and Gays in School*, City of Leicester Teachers' Association.

Colvin, M. (1989). *Section 28: A Practical Guide to the Law and its Implications*, London, Liberty.

DES (1984). *English 5–16*, London, HMSO.

——(1988a). *Sex Education at School: DES Circular 11/87*, London, Department of Education and Science.

——(1988b). *Local Government Act 1988: Section 28; DES Circular 88/90*, London, Department of Education and Science.

——(1989). *The National Curriculum: English for Ages 5 to 16*, London, Department of Education and Science.

Elbow, P. (1978). *Writing Without Teachers*, Oxford University Press.

Follett, R. J., and Larson, R. (1982). 'Bait/rebait: homosexuality', *English Journal*, 7, 4.

Foucault, M. (1981). *The History of Sexuality (An Introduction)*, Harmondsworth, Penguin.

Fricke, A. (1981). *Reflections of a Rock Lobster: A Story about Growing Up Gay*, Boston, Alyson Publications.

Galloway, B. (ed.) (1983). *Prejudice and Pride*, London, Routledge & Kegan Paul.

Garden, N. (1982). *Annie on My Mind*, New York, Farrar, Straus & Giroux.

Gay Teachers' Group (1987). *School's Out*, London, Gay Teachers' Group.

Gide, A. (1985). *Corydon*, London, Gay Men's Press.

Greater London Council, in co-operation with the GLC Gay Working Party (1985). *Changing the World: A London Charter for Gay and Lesbian Rights*, Greater London Council.

——(1986). *Tackling Heterosexism*, Greater London Council Women's Committee.

Hall, C. (1988). 'Young homosexuals: how we fail them', *Times Educational Supplement*, 15 January, p. 26.

Haringey Education Service (1988). *Mirrors around the Walls: Respecting Diversity*, London, Haringey Education Service.

Heron, A. (ed.) (1983). *One Teenager in 10: Writing by Gay and Lesbian Youth*, Boston, Alyson Publications.

Hirst, A. (1983). *Report*, PGCE dissertation, Institute of Education, London.

Howard, M. (1987). Speech reported in *Hansard*, 124, 65, 15 December.

ILEA (1983). *The English Curriculum: Race*, London, ILEA English Centre.

——(1984). *The English Curriculum: Gender*, London, ILEA English Centre.

——(1986). *Positive Images: A Resources Guide for Teaching about Homosexuality, including Lesbian and Gay Literature for Use in the Library and the Classroom*, Materiography no. 11, London, ILEA.

——(1988). *The English Curriculum: Class*, London, ILEA English Centre.

Industry and Employment Branch of the Greater London Council (1986). *Danger!*

Heterosexism at Work!, London, Industry and Employment Branch of the Greater London Council.

Ireland, T. (1984). *Who Lies Inside*, London, Gay Men's Press.

Jackson, A. (1987). 'Towards a school policy on homosexuality', *School's Out*, London, Gay Teacher's Group.

King, M. L. (1958). *Stride towards Freedom (The Montgomery Story)*, New York, Harper & Row.

Kinsey, A. C. *et al.* (1947). *Sexual Behaviour in the Human Male*, Saunders.

——(1953). *Sexual Behaviour in the Human Female*, Saunders.

Knott, R. (1985). *The English Department in a Changing World*, Milton Keynes, Open University Press.

LAGER (1989). *Education Employment Rights Information*, London, LAGER.

Lane, K. (1984). *Lesbians and Gays and Schooling*, PGCE dissertation, Institute of Education, London.

Lock, M. A. (1984). *Adolescence and Homosexuality: A Study of Teenage Sexual Orientation*, PGCE dissertation, Institute of Education, London.

London Diocesan Board for Schools (1979). *Lifestyles and Sexual Orientation: A Memorandum for Teachers and Governors in Church Schools*, London Diocesan Board for Schools.

McLeod, A. (1985). 'Accepted as natural?', *Teaching London Kids*, 23, 12–13.

Mars-Jones, A. (1987). 'Homosexual men as soft targets', *Spectator*, 15 August.

Medway, P. (1983). *Finding a Language: Autonomy and Learning in School*, London, Chameleon Books.

——(1986). 'What gets written about', in A. Wilkinson, *The Writing of Writing*, Milton Keynes, Open University Press.

Morin, S. F. and Garfinkle, E. M. (1978). 'Male homophobia', *Journal of Social Issues*, 34, 1, 29–47.

Morris, S. and Read, E. (1985). *Out in the Open*, London, Pan.

Mullen, P. (1987). 'Licensed to pervert', *Times Educational Supplement*, 16 October, p. 22.

Neave, T. (1988). 'Homosexuality and education', *Gay Times*, May 1988.

North London Lesbian Group (1988). *Heterosexism for Beginners*, North London Lesbian Group.

Olson, M. R. (1987). 'A study of gay and lesbian teachers', *Journal of Homosexuality*, 13, 4, Haworth Press.

Parker, R. (1986). 'Richard: an autobiography', *English in Education*, 20, 14–16.

Patrick, P. (1985). 'Trying hard to hear you', *Teaching London Kids*, 23, 7–11.

Place, M. (1981). *Queer Bashing: How the Mass Media and Peer Group Pressure Destroy the Emotional Well-being of the Gay Teenager*, PGCE dissertation, Institute of Education, London.

Protherough, R., Atkinson, J. and Fawcett, J. (1989). *The Effective Teaching of English*, London, Longman.

Sanderson, T. (1986). *How to be a Happy Homosexual*, London, The Other Way Press.

Slayton, P. and Vogel, B. (1985). 'People without faces; adolescent homosexuality and literature', *English and Education*, 20, 1, 5–13.

Stafford, J. M. (1987). 'Positive gay images', *Times Educational Supplement*, 16 October, p. 22.

——(1988). *Homosexuality and Education*, Manchester, J. Martin Stafford.

Stop the Clause Education Group (1989). *Section 28: A Guide for Schools, Teachers and*

Governors, London, Stop the Clause Education Group in association with All London Teachers Against Racism and Fascism.

Tingle, R. (1986). *Gay Lessons: How Public Funds are used to Promote Homosexuality among Children and Young People*, Pickwick Books.

Townley, C. (1989). *Positive Images of Lesbians and Gay Men in Teenage Fiction*, BEd dissertation, University of Cambridge.

Trenchard, L. and Finch, M. (1987). *Are we Being Served? Lesbians, Gays and Broadcasting Project Report*, London, Hall Carpenter Memorial Archives.

Trenchard, L. and Warren, H. (1984). *Something to Tell You*, London Gay Teenage Group.

Trevisan, J. (1986). *Perverts in Paradise*, London, Gay Men's Press.

Ustinov, P. (1977). *Dear Me*, Harmondsworth, Penguin.

Warren, H. (1984). *Talking about School*, London Gay Teenage Group.

Watkins, L. and Worcester, R. M. (1985). *Private Opinions – Public Polls*, London, Thames & Hudson.

Wolfenden Report (1957). *The Wolfenden Report: Report of the Committee on Homosexual Offences and Prostitution*. Cmnd 247, London, HMSO.

Index